B U G S Y

DATE DUE

WARREN BEATTY
as Benjamin "Bugsy" Siegel

ANNETTE BENING
as Virginia Hill

HARVEY KEITEL
as Mickey Cohen

BEN KINGSLEY
as Meyer Lansky

JOE MANTEGNA
as George Raft

BUGSY

AN ORIGINAL SCREENPLAY
BY JAMES TOBACK

A CITADEL PRESS BOOK
PUBLISHED BY CAROL PUBLISHING GROUP

791.4372
B8664X

A Citidel Press Book
Published by Carol Publishing Group
Citadel Press is a registered trademark of Carol Commmunications, Inc.
Editorial Offices: 600 Madison Avenue, New York, N.Y. 10022
Sales & Distribution Offices: 120 Enterprise Avenue, Secaucus, N.J. 07094
In Canada: Musson Book company, a division of General Publishing Company, Ltd., Don Mills, Ontario M3B2T6

Queries regarding rights and permissions should be addressed to
Carol Publishing Group, 600 Madison Avenue, N.Y. 10022

Carol Publishing Group books are available at special discounts for bulk purchases, for sales promotions, fund raising, or educational purposes. Special editions can be created to specifications. For details, contact: Special Sales Department, Carol Publishing Group, 120 Enterprise Avenue, Secaucus, N.J. 07094

Stills from BUGSY courtesy of TriStar Pictures, Inc.
Cover and Book Design: Eric Baker Design Associates, Inc.

Manufactured in the United States of America

10 9 8 7 6 5 4 3 2 1

Library of Congress Cataloging-in-Publication Data

Toback, James.
    Bugsy : the official publication of the blockbuster film :
screenplay / by James Toback.
        p.   cm.
    ISBN 0-8065-1288-1
    I. Title
PN1997.B792   1991   91-34166
791.43'72—dc20   CIP

c -1

ACKNOWLEDGMENTS

To Stephanie Kempf who did the first research, organizing chaos into a shape which yielded hope, and to Warren Beatty and Barry Levinson who went far beyond the roles of actor and director in their constant inspiration.

Producers Barry Levinson (with cap), Warren Beatty, and Mark Johnson discuss an upcoming desert scene as Annette Bening watches from behind the wheel of the car.

FOR SELMA L. TOBACK

WHO FROM THE START HAS LACKED NOTHING AND GIVEN EVERYTHING

INTRODUCTION

In 1984, that Orwellian landmark so far removed from the present that I still had something resembling a full head of hair, Warren Beatty, my friend and sometime cocreator (he worked with me on two of the films that I wrote and directed—*Love and Money* and *The Pick-up Artist*) approached me with an offer. He would provide me with some much needed front money in return for an original screenplay about Benjamin "Bugsy" Siegel. I could not have invented a happier way out of the debt in which I had ensconced myself. I had—from the first time I saw Beatty (in *Splendor in the Grass* and *Mickey One*)—been drawn to him more than to any other screen presence of the time, drawn in that mysterious, irrational, invasive way peculiar to one's sense of certain film stars, which is to say that their pull is unconditional and transcendent of one's conventional notion of acting talent. One would rather see a mediocre movie, often even a bad one, featuring a star who has this hold, than a first-rate film populated by excellent actors who, however, could never quite touch that nether region of one's consciousness.

But my excitement was not stirred only by Beatty. As a role to construct for him to embody, none could have appealed to me so quickly or so deeply as that of Bugsy Siegel, whose range of incarnations—gangster, lover, inventor, killer, husband, visionary, gambler, Jew— is as broad as any public figure's in the era between the wars. So I accepted the offer readily, cashed the check, and committed myself to deliver a final draft in three months.

Six years later—having made two movies in between—I sent Beatty my script. To this day I cannot confidently explain the comic (to an outsider, if not to Beatty or to me) lateness of my delivery. Perhaps it was my intuition that Beatty, who had refused my request to tie me in from the beginning as the director of *Bugsy*, was not ever going to go along with that idea. Perhaps it was the pleasure that I took in absorbing, with my researcher, Stephanie Kempf, the stacks of books, newspaper and magazine accounts, and video and film records of the period. Or perhaps it was just an inexplicable perversity, an undertow of self-sabotage (a trait Bugsy himself wore like a badge of identity).

Whatever the explanation, the script was finally completed in mid-1990. I had written about twenty previous drafts over the six years, but the more time went by, the more pressure I felt to have the draft I finally showed ready to put in preproduction. (No script, even if the writer is going to direct, produce, and act in it as well, is ever ready to shoot as is without first being bent and reshaped to the rigors of discussion and rehearsal with actors and to the realities of discovering locations.)

There was still the question of who the director would be. It was not entirely realistic to assume that, having written and directed a number of films—*Fingers, Exposed, The Pickup Artist, The Big Bang*—each of which had inspired its share of eloquent supporters but none of which had made anybody rich, I would be placed in charge of a movie that would cost a minimum of thirty million dollars. In addition, there was Beatty's Third Intelligence Theory of Moviemaking. (Essentially, the idea is that three people deciding the course of a movie are better than two, since when there are two, one always emerges as the stronger and the film is left without a sufficiently tense dialectic, whereas when there are three, every idea needs to pass rigorous scrutiny.) So I should not have been surprised when Beatty, whose decision it was, by dint of the advance he paid me, told me that he had offered the script to Barry Levinson, who had directed *Rain Man* and *Good Morning, Vietnam*, two of the most commercially successful movies ever made.

And, indeed, I wasn't surprised. I was shocked. Bugsy lived in my consciousness and my system. I had written him, however belatedly, from the inside out, and no one could direct my vision, my script, except me. Levinson would have to go. As there was little chance of voluntary departure, I would have to resort to a method Bugsy would have understood—a method he employed with startling frequency for a fundamentally sweet Jewish boy from Williamsburg: murder. I would, of course, be a suspect. But having established myself in advance as a colleague and friend (which I would cunningly do), I would ultimately walk, a free man, and the attendant publicity would only add to the movie's stature as a major sociocultural event.

Fortunately for the film and for my own future freedom and for Levinson's future as well, when I met him my affection for him was immediate and profound, and Beatty's Third Intelligence Theory proved strikingly apt. Each of us by turns stimulated the best in the other two, and each came to rely on the others to confirm and to provoke.

Over a four month preproduction period, I wrote seven new drafts and then rewrote and invented new lines, moments, and scenes daily during the three months of shooting. Characters who had seemed integral were banished into oblivion; the opening section, in New York (before Bugsy comes to Hollywood and then dreams up Las Vegas), was radically condensed. Connections between personality and fate, humor and tragedy, romance and death, were heightened and refined. There was a wonderful edge of anticipation every day, an intuition that each revision was moving us into an ever darker, wilder, funnier world.

There was in the historical Bugsy—and therefore necessarily in our fictional rendition of him—an extravagant mixture of personal charm and naïve megalomania. Indeed, one could propose that Bugsy's charm was indivisible from his megalomania. Levinson, Beatty, and I accepted this paradox as a fundamental part of his character which freed us of any temptation to ask the sort of reductive questions (Will the audience identify with our protagonist? Whom can we root for? Is he a "good" person?) that have infected discourse in and around commercial American movies for the past fifteen years.

I still look at writing without directing—at least in theory—as seduction without making love, but when I saw the rough cut of *Bugsy* last week, I was forced to conclude what I had imagined throughout shooting; that the collaboration had resulted in a film closer to the spirit and letter of my own script than I alone as a director—without Levinson—would have been able to provide. A script is a work in progress, the beginning of a journey—a blueprint and a guide. It is not, like the novel, story, poem, or even drama, a work contained and complete, the final enactment of the vision. But a script can, in rare cases, come tantalizingly close, so that what one sees and hears in one's mind and writes on the page fuse with what was performed and recorded and photographed, the latter an umbilical extension of the former, rather than a parallel version of it. For me, lucky and grateful, *Bugsy* is that extension, the word made reel.

New York
August 19, 1991

BUGSY

THE SCREENPLAY

EXT. BUGSY SIEGEL'S SCARSDALE MANSION - DAWN

BUGSY SIEGEL, dressed in a dark suit, heads out from his house toward his Cadillac parked in the driveway. It is a white winter dawn.

BARBARA, 11, and MILLICENT, 8, Bugsy's two daughters, chase him down and pull at him. Bugsy hugs them on his way to the car. ESTA, Bugsy's wife, has come out onto the lawn in a bathrobe and waves good-bye to Bugsy as he kisses Barbara and Millicent before driving away.

BUGSY

Six o'clock at the station.

MILLICENT & BARBARA

Bye...Bye...Bye, Daddy!

EXT. BUGSY'S CADILLAC - HENRY HUDSON PARKWAY - DAY

Bugsy drives past a lake. It is 1944. While driving, he reads from a book on elocution.

BUGSY

(to himself, repetitively)

In order to speak properly one must enunciate every syllable correctly: Twenty dwarves took turns doing handstands on the carpet...Twenty dwarves took turns doing handstands on the carpet.

INT. HOTEL - LOBBY - DAY

As Bugsy walks through the lobby, heads turn. The hall is well populated by a generally elegant and prosperous group. Bugsy nods, waves, and smiles at the various uniformed hotel employees, all of whom clearly know and like him. Entering the elevator, he notices JUNE, a striking woman of twenty-two.

INT. HOTEL ELEVATOR - DAY

Eight people, including Bugsy and June, stand in the elevator as the door closes.

ELEVATOR OPERATOR

How are you this afternoon, Mr. Siegel?

BUGSY

Better than I was about ten seconds ago.

Bugsy's answer is clearly meant to refer to June, with whom he shares a look.

ELEVATOR OPERATOR

(to June)

Floor, please, madam.

June doesn't answer.

BUGSY

Penthouse.

INT. PENTHOUSE HALLWAY - HOTEL - DAY

June gets out and Bugsy follows. June waits to see which penthouse suite Bugsy will approach. Bugsy doesn't move; he just looks at June.

JUNE

Didn't anyone ever tell you that it's not polite to stare?

Bugsy continues to look at June.

Warren Beatty as Benjamin "Bugsy" Siegel

BUGSY

If we make love now, it'll be the only time.

JUNE

What if you like it?

BUGSY

Oh, I know I'll like it.

JUNE

Then why wouldn't you—

BUGSY

I don't know.

JUNE

I think I got off on the wrong floor.

Bugsy goes toward the elevator.

BUGSY

Then you better get back *on*.

As Bugsy reaches for the call button, June's hand gently diverts his, stopping him.

INT. BUGSY'S BEDROOM - PENTHOUSE SUITE - HOTEL - DAY

As Bugsy dresses in shirt, suit, and tie, he speaks on the phone.

BUGSY

(into the phone)

Meyer!…Relax!…Half an hour. Maximum… Of course I'm alone… *What* woman? That was an hour ago… I *have* thought it over and I *must* do it. You better wake up Charlie. You know he always likes to take a nap before a little trouble.

EXT. NEW YORK STREET - DRIVING - NIGHT

We are tight on Bugsy, MEYER LANSKY (in the middle seat) and CHARLIE LUCIANO (in the window passenger seat) as the black Lincoln moves through moderate midtown traffic. Throughout Meyer and Charlie's dialogue, Bugsy just listens, silently amused.

MEYER

Ben, I gotta tell you once again that it really does affect my opinion of your ability to administrate when you involve yourself in this type of detail.

> (to Charlie)

Charlie. Tell him what you said to me when I told you about it.

CHARLIE

What do you *think* I said to you?

MEYER

> (to Bugsy)

You see what I'm talking about?

> (to Charlie)

And then you just shook your head.

CHARLIE

Of course I shook my head. What else was I gonna do?

Bugsy pulls up to the curb in front of a dry-cleaning store.

BUGSY

Count to fifty-three.

Carrying a gift-wrapped Sulka's box, Bugsy gets out of the car.

INT. J. GRIMALDI CLEANERS - NIGHT

Bugsy enters and walks past DAVE the counterman.

DAVE

Good evening, Mr. Siegel...

BUGSY

> (throws his hat to Dave)

Hi, Dave. Give it a quick brush for me, will you?

DAVE

Sure.

INT. J. GRIMALDI CLEANERS - STEAM PRESS ROOM - NIGHT

Bugsy moves through the room, past the steam presses. He opens the door to reveal a bookmaking operation.

Bugsy moves through lines of clothes to the back of the store.

Bugsy pays a visit to J. Grimaldi Cleaners to settle a business matter

INT. BOOKMAKING SHOP - NIGHT

Five MEN WORKERS, busy on the phones, write horse bets. They are separated by a glass partition from JERRY, fat, in a suit, who is counting a stack of hundred dollar bills while eating (sloppily) a massive Chinese meal. He isn't aware of Bugsy's entrance until Bugsy is nearly on top of him.

> **BUGSY**
>
> Hi, Jerry.

> **JERRY**
>
> Ben! What are you doing here? I thought you was on your way to California.

> **BUGSY**
>
> I am on my way to California. I just came to give you a good-bye present.

Bugsy hands Jerry the gift-wrapped box.

> **JERRY**
>
> A present?

The workers notice Bugsy and Jerry but can't hear.

> **BUGSY**
> (to Jerry)
>
> Open it.

Jerry warily opens the box and finds the shirts and ties.

> **JERRY**
>
> I don't get it.

> **BUGSY**
>
> Meyer, Charlie, and I hire you to do a job, we pay you a salary, we throw in a piece of the action, and you return the favor...by stealing from us for the second time in three years.

> **JERRY**
>
> Stealing?

> **BUGSY**
>
> Yeah, stealing. The shirt off my back. You want the shirt off my

back? I'll give you the shirt off my back! Here—from Sulka's—the same ones *I* wear.

J E R R Y

Could I say something, Ben?

B U G S Y

I'm in a bit of a rush or I would have bought you some jackets, pants, suits, and shoes. But I can give you a couple of tips.

EXT. J. GRIMALDI CLEANERS - STREET - CAR - NIGHT

Meyer and Charlie sit impatiently.

C H A R L I E

Thirty-nine hundred dollars we pay to hire three guys to take care of this problem.

M E Y E R

What am I gonna tell you, Charlie, his thinkin' process?

C H A R L I E

So now all of a sudden this madman decides he's gotta jump in and do it by himself.

INT. BOOKMAKING SHOP - NIGHT

Bugsy presses different shirts against Jerry's torso—deftly changing ties as well—in an effort to find the right combination. Jerry is confused and on the verge of terror.

B U G S Y

See, now this you can wear with a blue blazer and gray flannel pants. But no double-breasteds. They expand the middle. You gotta lose fifty pounds before you go double-breasted.

J E R R Y

Ben—

B U G S Y

And I'll tell you something else—don't listen to the people who tell you that you can't wear suede shoes with flannel...not only can you wear suede, you can wear *brown* suede! Let me see your shoes. Jerry! I don't want to be rude—but they don't go with anything.

EXT. J. GRIMALDI CLEANERS - STREET - CAR - NIGHT

MEYER

The way I see it, Charlie, Ben has only one problem…the same problem he's had since we were all kids together stickin' up crap games on the streets — he doesn't respect money.

CHARLIE

I'm gonna take a nap.

Charlie closes his eyes.

INT. BOOKMAKING SHOP - NIGHT

Bugsy, shirts and ties strewn all over the table, finally gestures triumphantly as he presses a yellow tie against a pink shirt (both spread across Jerry's chest).

BUGSY

Now if you blend this combination with an elegant beige linen jacket with cream-colored pleated pants and white shoes — but that's for summer. And you don't have to worry about summer.

Bugsy pulls his gun out of his pocket and aims it at Jerry.

JERRY

Oh, Ben, don't…

BUGSY

I'm sorry Jerry, I can't keep my friends waiting any longer. I'm sure they're already getting a little impatient with me. It's just business to them. If it were just business to me, I'd be selling insurance or importing dresses.

Bugsy fires five shots into Jerry, who falls back in his chair in a heap, the blood saturating his new shirts. Bugsy looks at the corpse, then at the workers who watch, stunned, through the glass partition, and then look down and continue their work. Bugsy makes his way through the dry cleaner's steam.

INT. GRAND CENTRAL STATION - PLATFORM - NIGHT

The steam of the trains. People are boarding the train for California. The dining car is guarded at either end by both uniformed Pullman personnel and beefy gangsters, two of each at both entrances.

INT. PULLMAN TRAIN - LOUNGE CAR - NIGHT

A strategy session, directed at Bugsy (who is smiling to himself and whose mind seems elsewhere) is in progress. Meyer, Charlie, JOEY A. (Adonis), FRANK COSTELLO, ALBERT ANASTASIA, WILLIE MORETTI, MOE SEDWAY, WHITEY KRAKOWER, HARRY GREENBERG, VITO GENOVESE, GUS GREENBAUM, and Bugsy are seated with a buffet of food and drink.

Throughout, Bugsy is attentive and relaxed. He smokes a cigar and sips a J&B.

CHARLIE

Ben. Lookit. We're sendin'…sendin' you to knock out Jack Dragna and take over the Southern California rackets. But you gotta approach him amiable. You gotta make it look like all you want is to come in as a partner.

MEYER

The guy has been running the rackets in Southern California for twenty years with no competition.

MOE

Except for Mickey Cohen, who you don't even count because he's a one-man gang.

MEYER

So the only way to move in on Dragna is…amiably.

FRANK

Offer him a better deal than the one he's got with Trans-National.

MEYER

Yeah. He pays rent there. We offer him to own a wire. Fifty-fifty. We put up cash and use his people. Down the road we shift it fifty-one/forty-nine. From there it's ours. But you gotta open amiably.

VITO

What about the gambling joints he's got and the —

MEYER

Vito, I just said it's fifty-fifty.

MOE

Fifty-fifty.

MEYER

We move in but we don't ruin anything by being too crazy.

MOE

Just be amiable.

CHARLIE

Joey A. knows Jack Dragna personally.
(to Joey A.)
What do you think, Joey?

JOEY A.

Jack Dragna's a cold-blooded killer. You gotta be very careful with him. So don't say nothin' he could take offense at.
(Bugsy smiles)
What are you smilin' at?

BUGSY

Nothing.

INT. BUGSY'S COMPARTMENT - NIGHT

Esta, Millicent, and Barbara sit patiently waiting for Bugsy. Esta removes the silver-covered dome from the plate.

ESTA

You girls should start eating before it gets too cold.

INT. PULLMAN TRAIN - LOUNGE CAR - NIGHT

MEYER

Ben. When you get to Los Angeles, do us all a favor. Don't call George. I know he's a good friend of yours but he's such a big shot movie star now he attracts more attention than Franklin Delano Roosevelt. The whole trip's gotta be quick and quiet.

BUGSY

And amiable.

MEYER

That's right.

Meyer gets Bugsy's tease in a delayed reaction and is amused by it in spite of himself.

M E Y E R

Very funny.

(they share a smile)

Twelve days. Four days out, four days of diplomacy, four days back. No one even knows you were there.

They embrace. On Bugsy's way out, Harry approaches him.

H A R R Y

Could I have a word with you alone, Ben?

B U G S Y

After I say good-bye to my family.

EXT. GRAND CENTRAL STATION - PLATFORM - NIGHT

Bugsy kisses Esta, Millicent, and Barbara good-bye.

B U G S Y

Four days out, four days in, four days back.

E S T A

We'll see you in twelve days.

B U G S Y

Twelve days exactly. And I'll miss you every minute I'm gone.

E S T A

I'll miss you, Ben.

B U G S Y

(to Millicent and Barbara)

Millicent, Barbara, when I call you on the phone I want both of you to tell me what presents you want me to bring back.

B A R B A R A

I know already. I want —

B U G S Y

Don't tell me now. Think about it. Then surprise me.

INT. BUGSY'S COMPARTMENT - NIGHT

Bugsy sits down in front of the sunlamp. Harry sits behind him on the couch.

> **HARRY**
>
> I need money, Ben.

> **BUGSY**
>
> How much?

> **HARRY**
>
> Fifty thousand dollars.

> **BUGSY**
>
> For what?

> **HARRY**
>
> The cops, the D.A., the F.B.I. They're threatenin' to lock me up. They're no good, these people. Except for this one Assistant D.A., Allen Stein. Jewish kid. Nice fella. You know his family from Bedford Street.

> **BUGSY**
>
> What happened to the fifty thousand I just gave you, Harry?

> **HARRY**
>
> What fifty thousand?

> **BUGSY**
>
> The fifty thousand for the armored truck heist.

> **HARRY**
>
> *That* fifty thousand? That fifty thousand is gone, Ben. You know me with money. I blew it at the track.

The train starts to move.

Bugsy spins around to face Harry.

> **BUGSY**
>
> What are you saying, Harry? Are you saying that if I don't give you fifty thousand dollars, you're going to rat on everyone you know, including me?

HARRY

You? Never! I love you, Ben. I would never rat on you…Never.

The train moves faster. Bugsy reaches over to the inside pocket of his jacket (on a hanger).

HARRY

(tentatively)

You ain't gonna kill me, Ben, are you?

Bugsy removes packets of cash from his pocket and hands it to Harry.

BUGSY

I'm going to try hard to forget this ever happened.

HARRY

I owe you my life, Ben.

BUGSY

I'd say that's a fair assessment.

HARRY

God bless you, Ben!

BUGSY

Bend your knees, Harry.

HARRY

Bend my knees?

BUGSY

When you jump from the train, bend your knees to soften the impact.

INT. UNION STREET RAILROAD STATION - TRACK 8 - DAY

GEORGE RAFT stands on the platform as the train pulls in. Autograph seekers — as well as fans who just want to say a word or shake his hand — continue to approach him. Bugsy and a PORTER carrying four suitcases climb down from the train. Bugsy exchanges a look of shared pleasure with CARLA, an attractive woman who is alighting from the train.

CARLA

This has been four of the most wonderful days I've ever spent.

BUGSY

A lot of it was the motion of the train.

She smiles and walks off. Bugsy gets caught in the crowd.

A fan sees George wave to Bugsy — who at this point sees George.

FAN

He *knows* you. Are you somebody too?

BUGSY

Nah.

George, surrounded by his newfound entourage, comes face to face with Bugsy.

GEORGE

Ben! Gee, you're looking great. Like a million bucks of real money.

BUGSY

You look pretty cute yourself, Georgie Boy. And very dapper.

GEORGE

That's what they pay me for.

INT. UNION STATION - DAY

Bugsy and George walk through Union Station.

GEORGE

I was so excited when you called from Flagstaff to say you were coming.

BUGSY

What did you think? That I was going to come to Los Angeles and not see my best old buddy the minute I arrived?

GEORGE

I've got you registered in the Beverly Hills Hotel. Bungalow 5. I know you said four days but I made the reservation for six, just in case.

George hands a key to Bugsy, who puts it in his pocket.

George Raft (Joe Mantegna, center) obliges the autograph seekers as he goes to meet boyhood pal Bugsy Siegel's train

EXT. HOLLYWOOD BOULEVARD - DRIVING - DAY

Bugsy and George are driving.

BUGSY

So Jack Dragna is the kingpin out here. What do you hear about him?

GEORGE

From what I hear, he runs a n ce little operation.

BUGSY

He's got a city here with three million people in it and he runs an operation that's nice and little.

GEORGE

Less to worry about. I'm gonna drop you off at the hotel and then I've gotta run back to the studio.

BUGSY

Why don't I go over there with you?

GEORGE

All right if you like.

BUGSY

Jack Dragna, nice and little.

EXT./INT. STAGE 11 - WARNER BROS. LOT - DAY

Bugsy enters George's stage. In a state of utter fascination and delight, he wanders about the stage, transfixed by both the technical mechanics and the separate pockets of activity (makeup and hair, clothes, design plans, lighting, sound systems).

BUGSY

This place is...spectacular!

George approaches Bugsy.

GEORGE

Take one of these chairs. I think you'll find this interesting.

BUGSY

I think I will.

George Raft crosses the movie lot on his way to the set...

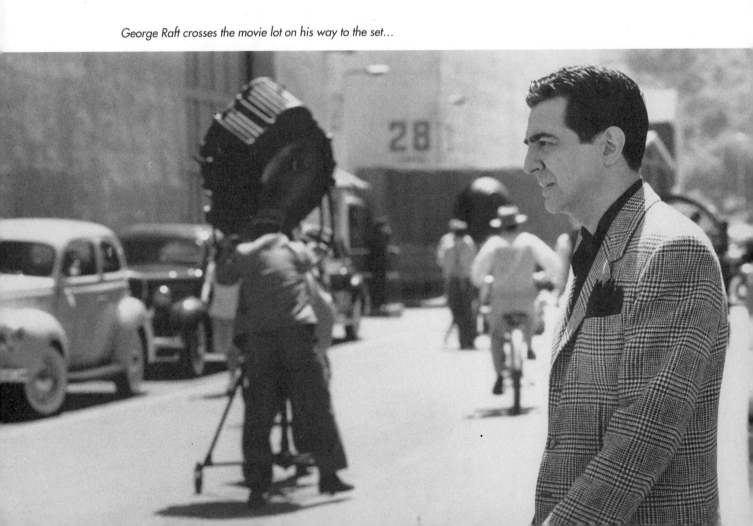

B U G S Y

A series of jump cuts of George and MARLENE from different angles doing their scene from *Manpower* is intercut with Bugsy—fascinated by what he is seeing—and snippets of other appropriate sounds and words (e.g. "speed," "action," "cut," and, finally, "That's a wrap.").

> **MARLENE**
>
> You've got a lot of gall crawling in here and setting yourself up as the old family lawyer. I don't know whether to laugh in your face or to bat it in with a bottle.

> **GEORGE**
>
> I'd stick to the laughin' if I were you. I duck fast and swing faster. Hank ain't very bright but he's my friend and if he hooks up with a dame like you he's tying himself into a lot of headaches he never figured on. I'm onto your racket.

George pulls a large roll of money from his pants pocket.

> **MARLENE**
>
> Now you take that money and stick it back in your pocket. Go and buy yourself some manners.

> **GEORGE**
>
> For what? To waste on you?

> **MARLENE**
>
> Now listen, mister. Before you came in here I was worrying about Hank. I figured I wouldn't marry him because he's a regular guy. And he's been swell to me. But now I'm gonna marry him whether you like it or not. Is there anything else?

> **GEORGE**
>
> No. Check.

> **MAITRE D'**
>
> What's the trouble, folks?

> **MARLENE**
>
> Oh, this muzzler's trying to buy up my spare time.

> **GEORGE**
> (perusing the check)
> Two bucks for what? One beer and some phony champagne?

31

...where he does a scene from Manpower with Marlene Dietrich (Ksenia Prohaska)

Bugsy arrives on the Warner Bros. lot to visit with George Raft...

MAITRE D'

That's right, friend.

GEORGE

Here's half a buck. Split it between ya.

MAITRE D'

Ain't you bein' a little hasty, pal?

MARLENE

The tinhorns that talk biggest scream the loudest when they get the check. You're so cheap you're wholesale.

MAITRE D'

Those are our prices, chum...Cash on the line.

GEORGE

Four bits. That's all it's worth. Dame and all.

MAITRE D'

(taking George by the lapels)

You don't want to get in no trouble, do ya?

GEORGE

I just had this suit pressed. Take your paws off it.

MAITRE D'

Ha, ha, ha.

GEORGE

Don't forget, mister, I asked you nice.

George punches the maitre d' in the jaw, then turns around and hits the man behind him. George keeps swinging, breaking a chair in order to use part of it as a bat to ward off attackers.

GEORGE

Boy, with this I could hit home runs all night.

He backs through the crowd, hitting several people on the way. He brushes VIRGINIA.

...and becomes captivated by the process of moviemaking

GEORGE

Here, take this in case I decide to come back.

We hear "cut" and a clap board "clap." The bell rings and shooting is completed. George hands Virginia the broken chair leg.

VIRGINIA

I think I need a line here.

George approaches an inspired Bugsy.

BUGSY

That was pretty impressive, Georgie boy.

As George responds and Bugsy counters, Bugsy notices—and is seized by—VIRGINIA HILL.

GEORGE

I'm a pro.

BUGSY

You certainly are.

Bugsy turns and walks with Virginia as she passes him, sticking a cigarette in her mouth.

BUGSY
(pulling out his lighter)

May I?

VIRGINIA
(sizing him up)
If you want a simple yes or no, you'll have to finish the question.

BUGSY

Light your cigarette.

Bugsy lights it.

VIRGINIA

The way you were staring at me, I thought you were gonna ask me for something a little more exciting.

BUGSY

Like what for instance?

Starlet Virginia Hill (Annette Bening) arrives on the set and while awaiting her call...

...meets Bugsy, sizes him up...

and strikes up an acquaintanceship

VIRGINIA

Use your imagination.

BUGSY

I'm using it.

Virginia turns and walks away. Bugsy looks at George.

BUGSY

You're not going to tell me she's a bit player.

GEORGE

Flamingo? Not to Joey Adonis. That's Virginia Hill.

BUGSY

That's Virginia Hill?

GEORGE

Don't get no ideas, Ben. You know how crazy Joey can get. No woman's worth a bullet between the eyes. Am I right or wrong?

BUGSY

Depends on whose eyes and which woman.

Bugsy moves swiftly and smoothly to Virginia and looks into her eyes.

VIRGINIA

Look, you're Ben Siegel and I'm Virginia Hill. Okay? Why are you interested in a gal who's going with your friend?

BUGSY

What friend? Joey A.? He's not my friend. He's the associate of an associate. You're still going with him?

VIRGINIA

If it were New Year's Eve, he would be my date.
                    (they share a look)
Who would your date be?

BUGSY

Wife.

VIRGINIA

Wife?

BUGSY

Esta.

VIRGINIA

Esther?

BUGSY

Esta. E-s-t-a.

VIRGINIA

Let me guess. I'll bet Esta lives her life faithful to her one and only Ben, who plays around like a jackrabbit on the side and lies about it through his teeth.

BUGSY

I don't lie to Esta.

VIRGINIA

That's noble. What do you do? Confess your sins three times a day or do you just say nothing because you know she'll never ask? Now what exactly does Mr. Esta really want from Miss Virginia?

BUGSY

Mr. Esta is having a great deal of difficulty trying to imagine anything he *doesn't* want from Miss Virginia.

VIRGINIA

Oh, I'm sure he could pull a rabbit out of his hat if he really tried. Are you ready for a divorce, Mr. Siegel?

BUGSY

Never.

VIRGINIA

Wow! You're pretty ferocious where Mom's concerned, aren't you? The rest of the time you're just another good-looking, sweet-talking, charm-oozing, fuck-happy fella with nothing to offer but some dialogue. Dialogue's cheap in Hollywood, Ben. Why don't you run outside and jerk yourself a soda.

Virginia turns and walks away from him. Bugsy is elated.

EXT. BEVERLY HILLS - RESIDENTIAL - DRIVING - DAY

BUGSY

Georgie, how would someone go about getting a screen test done up?

GEORGE

Why? You know somebody who wants a screen test?

BUGSY

No. No. I just thought…What about Virginia? You think she has a future in movies?

GEORGE

In movies? I don't know if *I've* got a future in movies.
(pointing out some homes)
Lana Turner lives there…Cesar Romero lives there… and Gary Cooper is up the street. He paid forty-five thousand for that place.

BUGSY

Yeah? Houses go for that kind of money here?

GEORGE

Sure. And more.

Bugsy points to a house.

BUGSY

Whose is that?

GEORGE

Uh…Lawrence…What's his name… the opera singer.

BUGSY

Melchior?

GEORGE

No, no…the other one.

BUGSY

What other one?

GEORGE

Uh…What's his name?

BUGSY

Tibbett? Lawrence Tibbett?

GEORGE

Tibbett! That's it.

BUGSY

Stop for a second. That house is owned by Lawrence Tibbett?

Bugsy opens his door, forcing George to pull to a sharp stop. Bugsy gets out.

GEORGE

What are you doin'?

BUGSY

Paying my respects.

EXT. BEVERLY HILLS STREET - TIBBETT'S HOUSE - DAY

Bugsy walks to the door, knocks. An English Butler, RONALD, 75, greets him.

RONALD

Yes?

BUGSY

I'm looking for Lawrence Tibbett.

RONALD

Mr. Tibbett is in his study. May I tell him who's calling?

BUGSY

Ben Siegel.

RONALD

Is he expecting you?

BUGSY

Not unless he's psychic.

The Butler goes back inside. From what Bugsy can see from the door, he loves the house. He sprints back to the car.

EXT. BEVERLY HILLS STREET - DAY

BUGSY

How far is your house from here, Georgie?

GEORGE

Half a mile.

Bugsy removes a briefcase from the back seat.

GEORGE

What the hell are you doin', Ben?

EXT. TIBBETT'S HOUSE - DAY

Bugsy arrives carrying his briefcase. Tibbett comes to the door.

TIBBETT

Mr. Siegel...How can I help you?

BUGSY

Lawrence Tibbett! You have no idea what an honor and a thrill it is to meet you. I took my wife, Esta, and my two daughters to see you sing *Rigoletto* at the Met last year, and it was one of the great evenings of our lives.

TIBBETT

You overwhelm me, Mr. Siegel.

BUGSY

Ben.

TIBBETT

Ben Siegel. You wouldn't be related to *Bugsy* Siegel, would you?

BUGSY

"Bugsy"? What do you mean by "Bugsy"?

TIBBETT

I beg your pardon.

BUGSY

A bug is nothing. A bug does not exist. The word has no meaning. It's only used out of ignorance or malice. Do you know what a bug is? A "bug" is a colloquialism which has no basis in reality. Insects include a wide variety of living creatures that fly and crawl but none of them can be called a "bug." Are you following me? Because if you aren't —

TIBBETT

Yes. I am. I certainly didn't mean any offense, Mr. Siegel.

BUGSY

Ben.

TIBBETT

Ben.

BUGSY

May I take a look around, Larry?

TIBBETT

Of course. Be my guest.

BUGSY

You don't mind if I call you Larry?

TIBBETT

Not a bit. All my friends call me Larry.

INT. TIBBETT'S HOUSE - LIVING ROOM - DAY

Tibbett continues as he follows Bugsy into the living room.

TIBBETT

What brings you to Los Angeles, Ben?

BUGSY

Curiosity. This is a wonderful house, Larry. What do you think of the Beverly Hills Hotel?

TIBBETT

Best hotel in town. Is that where you're staying?

BUGSY

What do you prefer — the bungalows or the suites?

TIBBETT

The bungalows. Which one do you have?

BUGSY

None. You do.

(Bugsy hands Tibbett the key)

Bungalow Five.

TIBBETT

I don't understand.

BUGSY

I'm buying this house from you.

TIBBETT

Oh, this house isn't for sale.

BUGSY

Sure it is. Everything's for sale. How much you want for it?

TIBBETT

Mr. Siegel—

BUGSY

Ben.

TIBBETT

Ben, I…Why are you looking at me like that?

BUGSY

Like what?

TIBBETT

You're not going to hurt me, are you?

BUGSY

Hurt you? I would *protect* you from anyone who tried to hurt you. I *revere* you. Your voice helps to justify life. I'm just trying to give you money. How much do you want?

TIBBETT

For the house? But—

BUGSY

What'd you buy it for?

As Tibbett talks, Bugsy opens his briefcase and removes stacks of cash from it.

TIBBETT

Thirty-five thousand dollars. But that was a few years ago. I think I could get forty for it now. Maybe more. But even if…I mean, it's not really a financial issue, Mr. Siegel.

BUGSY

Ben.

TIBBETT

Ben. I—I—

Bugsy negotiates with opera star Lawrence Tibbett (Joe Baker) for the home Tibbett has no intention of selling

BUGSY

One…two…three…four…five. That's fifty thousand. Is that enough?

TIBBETT

Oh, it's more than —

BUGSY

Let's be sure. Let's make this a pleasant day for both of us. That's another ten. Sixty thousand. I feel sick inside when I don't bring pleasure to someone I admire. Does this bring you pleasure, Larry?

TIBBETT

Oh, my goodness, yes. But —

BUGSY

Then why don't I see you smiling.

TIBBETT

(tries to smile)

You have me flustered. You've paid too much. There are better houses for fifty thousand…just across the street.

BUGSY

When do you think I can move in?

TIBBETT

Next month? Would that be acceptable?

BUGSY

How about now? And we'll add another ten thousand.

Bugsy whips out another packet of ten thousand dollars and hands it to Tibbett.

BUGSY

You can pick up your things anytime you like. My house is yours.

EXT. BUGSY'S HOUSE—DAY

Bugsy and George are standing in front of Bugsy's house, inspecting it.

GEORGE

Jeez, Ben, the way you spend money, you'll never have anything left.

BUGSY

So? I'll make more. It's only dirty paper.

GEORGE

But what are you gonna do with a house, Ben? You're only gonna be in Los Angeles for four days.

BUGSY

Who knows? Maybe I'll stay a little longer. I've got to get to Jack Dragna's. Where can I get a taxi?

GEORGE

I'll drive you.

BUGSY

Uh-uh. This is business. I don't want you involved in any trouble. You don't want to be there.

EXT. LOS ANGELES STREET - DUSK

Bugsy rides in the back of a taxicab which stops at a traffic light. A chocolate-colored Cadillac convertible pulls up alongside. Bugsy looks at it admiringly, rolls down the window of the cab and speaks to the driver of the Cadillac.

BUGSY

Nice car.

CADILLAC DRIVER

Thank you.

EXT. JACK DRAGNA'S HOUSE - DUSK

Bugsy drives up to Jack's house in the Cadillac we've just seen him admiring.

He parks it and walks toward Jack's house. DOMINIC and LOUIE emerge and block Bugsy before he gets to the door.

LOUIE

What the hell is this?

BUGSY

I'm looking for Jack Dragna.

Bugsy meets with Jack Dragna (Richard Sarafian), who is running the rackets in Hollywood

LOUIE

Who the fuck are you?

BUGSY

Ben Siegel.

The two men look at each other, unsure.

LOUIE

I'm Louie, Jack's brother. I'll tell Jack you're here.

Louie goes inside.

INT. JACK DRAGNA'S HOUSE - LIVING ROOM - NIGHT

Bugsy paces as JACK DRAGNA, Louie, and Dominic sit, shifting uneasily and, finally, in disbelief.

BUGSY

So, you got three betting parlors in the entire city? What do they play—bridge?

JACK

Poker.

BUGSY

No blackjack? No craps? How about roulette? You got roulette? How about horse racing? What about the results? How do they get fed in?

JACK

Trans-National. Best wire service in the country.

BUGSY

From Chicago?

JACK

Right.

BUGSY

What do you pay for the service? Five hundred a day?

JACK

Thousand.

BUGSY

You take bets on sports?

JACK

Look, Mr. Siegel —

BUGSY

Ben.

JACK

We've got a smooth little operation out here. And with all due respect to you and Meyer Lansky and Charlie Luciano and Joey A. and whoever the fuck else you represent, I'd suggest that you spend your time in Los Angeles lookin' for broads, which we got plenty of the finest in the world and which I understand is right up your alley. Now there's a subject where I might be able to help you out — with phone numbers and whatnot. But if you're comin' lookin' to do business with me, I'm afraid I'm totally disinterested.

BUGSY

Un-interested.

JACK

What?

BUGSY

Disinterested means "impartial." *Un*interested means "not interested."

JACK

Whatever.

BUGSY

How many men do you have working for you?

JACK

Sixty-four.

BUGSY

You have two alternatives, Jack. You can take your sixty-four guys and start working for us. That means turning your smooth, little operation into a smooth, *big* one. It means twenty betting parlors instead of three, it means *owning* a wire service instead of subscribing to one, it means taking some risks. It means that Charlie and Meyer and I put up the front money and take seventy-five percent. You keep *twenty*-five, which should be worth about three times what your *hundred* percent is worth now.

JACK

What's the second alternative?

Bugsy whips out his pistol, startling everyone. He walks over to Jack with the pistol pointed at him only to reverse himself, twirling it and handing the pistol to Jack at the last moment.

JACK

What are you doin'? I don't need a gun. I got plenty of guns.

BUGSY

Take it.

Bugsy forces the pistol into Jack's hand and sets it so that Jack, in spite of himself, is aiming it straight at Bugsy.

BUGSY

Squeeze the trigger. Kill me.

JACK

What? *Kill* you? That's the second alternative?

Jack looks uneasy. Finally, he and his cohorts force laughter, a laughter which rides a crescendo to hysteria.

BUGSY

You guys have an unusual sense of humor. I missed the joke completely. Maybe it's the climate. What do you think?

JACK

I think what I heard about you is true. I think you're outta your fuckin' mind.

BUGSY

I'll give you another five seconds to make your selection.
    (Jack is mute)
I guess that means you're coming to work for us. It's a ball to have you on board.
    (Bugsy extends his hand)
May I have my gun back, please?
    (he takes the pistol from Jack)
Thank you. Let's get started. Time is vicious when you take it for granted.

Bugsy turns and starts toward the door.

LOUIE

    (calling out)
Hey!
    (Bugsy stops)
Bugsy! If we break off with Trans-National —

Bugsy turns around, looks at Louie, approaches him and then, suddenly and swiftly, flattens him with a powerful straight right, which cracks through his jaw.

BUGSY

I'll give you the benefit of the doubt — and assume you didn't know that no one calls me that.

Bugsy leaves.

JACK

That guy's fuckin' crazy.

LOUIE

You want me to run outside and shoot him in the back?

JACK

Yeah, sure. Then we can have Meyer Lansky and Charlie Luciano shootin' bullets up our ass.

LOUIE

So what do we do?

JACK

Wait. Play along. The guy's a hothead, and hotheads never last. Sooner or later he's gonna blow his lid. Then we can get him and no one will give a fuck.

EXT. JACK DRAGNA'S HOUSE - NIGHT

Bugsy is leaving Jack Dragna's house as we hear music fading in.

INT./EXT. HOLLYWOOD - MONTAGE

A Montage in which several elements are juxtaposed and intercut:

EXT. BUGSY'S PATIO

Bugsy sits in a lounge chair, sunning himself. He calls Virginia .

BUGSY

Hi!...Is this Virginia Hill? This is Ben Siegel—

Virginia hangs up.

BUGSY

Hello?

EXT. WARNER BROS. LOT

Bugsy calls Virginia from a phone booth on the Warner Bros. lot.

BUGSY

Hello, Virginia? This is Ben. Now don't hang up—

INT. BILTMORE HOTEL - LOBBY

Bugsy calls Virginia, but she hangs up.

INT. BILTMORE HOTEL - MURAL ROOM

Bugsy calls Virginia, but she hangs up.

INT. VIRGINIA'S HOUSE

Virginia answers the phone, but hangs up when she finds out it is Bugsy.

INT. BUGSY'S HOUSE - DAY

Bugsy, refurbishing and transforming Tibbett's house into his own, speaks on the phone as movers work around him.

> **BUGSY**
>
> Meyer, I know we said twelve days, but it's becoming a bit more complicated...I don't know...Two weeks, two months...The point is, this place is a gold mine.

INT. BETTING PARLOR

Bugsy supervises the setting up of betting operations. We see all forms of gambling—roulette, blackjack, craps, poker, races and sports betting.

EXT. WARNER BROS. - BACKSTAGE - VESTIBULE - NIGHT

Bugsy watches as the maitre d' from *Manpower* kisses Virginia good-bye and then slips out of her dressing room.

INT. BUGSY'S HOUSE

Bugsy plays George's role in the bar scene from *Manpower* for the camera (after a clap board signifies the making of a screen test). Ronald, who edges on camera accidentally for one line, plays the roles of the maitre d' and Marlene.

EXT. ARMORED CAR - NIGHT

Bugsy sets up an armored-car robbery and organizes various criminal activities.

At Ciro's, the Countess Dorothy di Frasso (Bebe Neuwirth) introduces Bugsy to her husband

INT. BUGSY'S HOUSE

Bugsy and George watch gangster movies (with Ronald as the projectionist).

INT. HOLLYWOOD - CIRO'S - NIGHT

Bugsy dancing at Ciro's with various partners.

INT. HOLLYWOOD - CIRO'S - NIGHT

Bugsy is the center of attention. We see Virginia on the other side of the dance floor talking to an OFFICER IN UNIFORM and watch Bugsy as he dances with the COUNTESS DOROTHY DI FRASSO. Bugsy's conversation is rhythmically connected to the beat of the music.

> **DOROTHY**
>
> I don't think I've ever danced with a real-life gangster before.

> **BUGSY**
>
> I've never danced with a countess before.

> **DOROTHY**
>
> You dance like an angel! Do you do everything else this well?

> **BUGSY**
>
> That changes with the partner.

> **DOROTHY**
>
> I'll take that as a challenge.

The dance ends. The patrons give Bugsy and Dorothy a huge response. Bugsy turns to one of the photographers who has been shooting him.

> **BUGSY**
>
> How was that?

> **PHOTOGRAPHER**
>
> Great.

> **BUGSY**
>
> You're from the *Examiner*?

> **PHOTOGRAPHER**
>
> Yeah.

B U G S Y

You think you can get them to print a flattering picture instead of all those sinister mug shots they always use? I'd appreciate it.

The COUNT DI FRASSO (who speaks with an Italian accent) approaches Dorothy.

C O U N T

May I have the honor of the next dance?

D O R O T H Y

I would be charmed. Have you met Mr. Siegel?

C O U N T

Not formally. But I've been admiring his movements.

D O R O T H Y

(to Bugsy)

This is my husband, the Count Di Frasso.

B U G S Y

I'm surrounded by titles. How can *I* pick one up?

C O U N T

A title?

B U G S Y

I'm beginning to feel left out.

D O R O T H Y

Darling. Get him a title. Let's make him a duke.

C O U N T

Why not? Are you ready to go to Italy, Mr. Siegel?

B U G S Y

Italy? I'll get my parachute.

C O U N T

(laughing uproariously)

Wonderful. Wonderful.

The Count puts his arm around Dorothy and starts to dance with her. George approaches Bugsy, whispers.

George Raft displays his smooth technique on the dance floor at Ciro's...

GEORGE

You know who one of the laughing count's best friends is?
Mussolini!

BUGSY

No.

GEORGE

Yeah.

BUGSY

(watching the Count)

That clown knows Mussolini? What do you think they *do* when
they're together? Play golf? Trade jokes about carting people off
to gas chambers?

GEORGE

You know me, Ben. I stay out of politics.

BUGSY

This isn't politics. It's war. The guy is Hitler's partner. Our mortal enemy. And this effete count pals around with him!

GEORGE

Take it easy, Ben. No sense in getting all worked up over something you can't do anything about. This is Hollywood.

It is at this point that Bugsy sees Virginia. Their eyes meet. He smiles. She would like to turn away but can't. A waiter, TONY, comes over to Bugsy, interrupting his moment. The officer starts dancing with Virginia, drawing her temporarily out of Bugsy's view.

TONY

Mr. Siegel? There's a telephone call for you. A Mr. Dragna. I have placed the phone at your table.

BUGSY

Thanks.

As Bugsy starts to his table, George stops him.

...before seeking out Bugsy to introduce him to District Attorney James McWilde (Bruce E. Morrow)

GEORGE

Ben, have you met our number-one crime fighter, James McWilde?

BUGSY

I haven't had the pleasure.

GEORGE

Mr. McWilde is up for reelection as district attorney.

BUGSY

I know. I wish I could contribute in some way.

MCWILDE

Well, I don't want to be presumptuous, but you could get in touch with Donald Mitchell — he handles all the money.

BUGSY

Donald Mitchell. Have him call me in the morning.

GEORGE

Excuse me, gentlemen, but there are six women waiting to talk to me.

George walks away. Bugsy's eyes meet Virginia's as she dances with the officer.

BUGSY

Tell me, Mr. McWilde, you're a man of the world — what do you make of all the friends this character Mussolini has flitting around America?

MCWILDE

I had no idea that was the case. Are you talking about spies?

At this point, HARTMAN, the assistant district attorney, comes over and draws McWilde away.

HARTMAN

Come, Jim, the senator is ready to leave and he says he *must* have a word with you.

MCWILDE

(to Bugsy)

Keep me posted on this Mussolini business.

BUGSY

I will. We gotta do something about this.

As McWilde is led off, Bugsy's temporary eye contact with a dancing Virginia is interrupted by her partner's turning her away. Bugsy walks to his table, where Tony has brought a phone. He hands Tony a small box, indicates Virginia.

BUGSY

Give this to her.

Tony obliges.

BUGSY

(into the phone)

What is it, Jack?

JACK

(V.O.)

This cocksucker, Mickey Cohen, just robbed our Franklin Street gambling joint out of fifty-six thousand cash. I tell you, I'm gonna get him this time and I'm gonna chop him up.

BUGSY

I'll see you in a few minutes.

Bugsy hangs up, watches Virginia.

EXT./INT. BUGSY'S FRANKLIN STREET BETTING PARLOR - NIGHT

There is a massive street scene — a savings bond rally — replete with banners, flags and huge photographs of Mussolini and Hitler. A man is standing on a box speaking. There is also a band playing the "Washington Post March." People sign up for savings bonds. Bugsy decends to the betting parlor, interrogates Jack.

BUGSY

How do you know it was Mickey Cohen?

JACK

I know.

DOMINIC

It was him. Definitely.

LOUIE

Absolutely.

First !

Bugsy makes a late night stop at his betting parlor to investigate the robbery

DOMINIC

No question about it. We saw him with our own eyes.

BUGSY

You mean he came in and did it himself? In person?

LOUIE

Exactly.

DOMINIC

He had a mask on, but it was definitely him. You could tell by that square body and that voice he's got.

BUGSY

Was he alone?

LOUIE

Yeah, but he had a forty-five.

DOMINIC

Two forty-fives.

BUGSY

What you're telling me is that *one* guy robbed *five* guys of fifty-six thousand dollars in their own place of business, and got away scot-free.

LOUIE

He took us by surprise.

BUGSY

Looks that way.

Bugsy wanders over to the window and looks up at the rally in progress.

JACK

Don't worry about it. He'll be dead within twenty-four hours.

BUGSY

I don't want him dead.

JACK

What do you mean?

B U G S Y

I want to talk to him.
                    (Bugsy turns back, looks at Jack)
You said fifty-six thousand?

J A C K

Yeah.

B U G S Y

To the penny?

J A C K

                    (turning to Louie)
To the penny?

L O U I E

No. It was fifty-six and change. The exact figure we got ripped off
for was fifty-six, one forty-three. That's the figure exact.

Bugsy registers the answer, then looks back up through the window to the rally. He leaves.

EXT. BUGSY'S HOUSE—NIGHT

A shot of Bugsy's house with his living room light the only light on inside.

INT./EXT. BUGSY'S HOUSE - LIVING ROOM - NIGHT

As Bugsy speaks into the phone, his screen test (a reenactment of the George/Marlene bar scene)
plays in the background—with Ronald a momentarily mistaken on-camera intruder.

B U G S Y

Esta…look, maybe the best thing would be for us to stop thinking
about when *I'm* coming back to *Scarsdale* and start thinking about
when you and the girls will come here…As soon as possible.

Through the window Bugsy sees Virginia drive up and get out of her car.

The sight of her changes Bugsy's approach on the phone.

B U G S Y

On the other hand, I don't know if this is the best time to take the
kids out of school…Maybe we should wait a while longer and play
it by ear.…I know, honey. But we don't have to settle every detail

Coming home, Bugsy prepares to view his screen test

in one phone conversation…One way or another we'll be together before you know it…I love you too, Esta…Good night.

Bugsy hangs up the phone, pulls the drapes aside and goes through an extravagant series of gestures to demonstrate that he will be with her in a moment. Virginia hesitates, then heads toward the house. The screen test is ending.

> **BUGSY**
> (yells out)
> Ronald! Stop the projector! Ronald? Ronald! Turn off the projector. Ronald?

Bugsy continues calling out as he goes into the hallway.

INT. BUGSY'S HOUSE - HALLWAY - NIGHT

Bugsy opens the door for Virginia.

> **VIRGINIA**
> Am I coming at a bad time?

> **BUGSY**
> Not at all. Come in.

> **VIRGINIA**
> I don't want to interrupt your pantomime.

> **BUGSY**
> No. That was just —

> **VIRGINIA**
> —What were you watching?

INT. BUGSY'S HOUSE LIVING ROOM - NIGHT

Light flickers on the blank screen, casting Bugsy and Virginia into silhouette.

> **BUGSY**
> A newsreel. It's over. Come on in.
> (shifting gears)
> Was it too early to put a ring on your finger?

VIRGINIA

Nothing's too early that fits. Do you always carry a spare ring?

BUGSY

Would you ever have called me?

VIRGINIA

I was planning to wait a while.

BUGSY

How long?

VIRGINIA

Ten years.

BUGSY

Why?

VIRGINIA

I guess I figured that since all we're gonna do is bring each other misery and torment—

BUGSY

Why would we have to bring each other misery and torment?

VIRGINIA

Because we both want to get whatever we want whenever we want it and we both want everything.

BUGSY

Doesn't sound too promising, does it?

VIRGINIA

That's what I'm saying.

BUGSY

Then why did you come?

VIRGINIA

Well...it wasn't caution.

BUGSY

How's Joey A.?

VIRGINIA

We're in touch. Does that bother you?

BUGSY

Uh-huh.

VIRGINIA

Because of your conscience, or are you worried about screwing up your business?

BUGSY

I haven't thought it through that clearly.

VIRGINIA

If he knew I was here now, the only thing *he'd* be trying to think through is which one of us to shoot first.

BUGSY

Do you want to kiss me as much as I want to kiss you?

He comes close to kissing her.

VIRGINIA

How do you know I want to kiss you at all?
(Bugsy comes closer)
I really don't think we should go ahead with this…Do you?

BUGSY

Uh…huh…

VIRGINIA

Is that yes or no?

BUGSY

Both.

At the last second, just as Bugsy is about to kiss her, Virginia slips away. Bugsy follows her into the light from the projector. He pulls her back by the waist and turns her around. She slaps him hard across the face.

BUGSY

You pack quite a punch.

VIRGINIA

That wasn't a punch. It was a slap. If I'd punched you, you'd be stretched out on the floor.

BUGSY

I'm sure you're right. I'm sure you're right about everything. I'm sure you're right about the misery. I'm sure you're right about the torment. I'm sure you're right about what you want and when you'll get it…I'm sure…

VIRGINIA

Do you always talk this much before you do it?

BUGSY

No…I only…talk this much before I'm going to kill someone.

Virginia looks at him and then they kiss, two shadows on the screen.

INT. BUGSY'S HOUSE - BEDROOM - DAWN

Bugsy and Virginia lie next to each other, embracing, asleep. The phone is ringing. Bugsy picks it up, groggily.

BUGSY

Hello…Hi, Georgie boy. You got a hold of Mickey Cohen? Great! Tell him to meet us at the Biltmore Health Club at one o'clock. Pick me up at twelve?…Good.

Bugsy hangs up. Virginia crawls on top of Bugsy. They start kissing.

BUGSY

You still think we'll bring each other nothing but misery and torment?

VIRGINIA

With some distractions in between.

BUGSY

You call what we've been doing a "distraction"?

VIRGINIA

Uh-huh.

BUGSY

Well, thank you. The feeling is mutual.

VIRGINIA

Good. That's the way I like it.

INT. BILTMORE HEALTH CLUB - DAY

Bugsy is lying on a lounge chair under a sun lamp with cucumbers on his eyes and facial creams galore. His hair, saturated with olive oil, is slicked back under a stocking. He wears a terry-cloth robe. George, script in hand, sits in a chair next to him.

Bugsy repeats to himself —

BUGSY

(to himself)

Twenty dwarves took turns doing handstands on the carpet.
Twenty dwarves took turns doing handstands on the carpet

(to George)

What time is it?

GEORGE

One-thirty.

BUGSY

He's half an hour late. Who does this thieving little schmuck think he's fucking with?

MICKEY COHEN emerges into the shot.

MICKEY

Who's a little schmuck? Who're you referrin' to, you preening fruitcake?

GEORGE

Hi, Mickey.

MICKEY

You better show me some respect.

BUGSY

I think you have it backward, Mr. Cohen, don't you? If I may be so bold as to correct you. Unless your idea of showing a man respect is to rob his place of business.

At the Biltmore Health Club, Bugsy, with cucumbers on his eyes and facial cream galore, relaxes poolside while talking business with Mickey Cohen (Harvey Keitel, standing) and George Raft

MICKEY

Who said I robbed? Robbed what, you would-be smoothie? Everything I got is mine.

BUGSY

It's only yours because you stole it from me.

MICKEY

Watch your words. What's mine is mine. Everything I got, I'm keepin'.

BUGSY

I understand from Jack Dragna that you stole fifty-six thousand and change.

MICKEY

The lying fuck! It was forty-two, not fifty-six!

BUGSY

Forty-two!…I thought you didn't steal *anything*.

MICKEY

I didn't. But if I had, it would've been forty-two.

Bugsy takes the cucumbers off his eyes and looks at Mickey.

BUGSY

If I were you, I'd give that money back by seven o'clock tonight.

MICKEY

If I was you, I'd shut my fuckin' mouth and watch my step. Or would you like me to blow your Adam's apple down your spine?

BUGSY

Excuse me, but aren't we in a public place? Maybe both of us would be better off if you toned down your rhetoric a notch.

MICKEY

Maybe we'd both be better off if I left you altogether and never saw your fuckin' face again.

Mickey storms out. As George shakes his head, Bugsy cracks up.

GEORGE

What are you laughin' at, Ben? The guy's deranged.

Bugsy leans over to the phone and starts dialing.

BUGSY

Go get him. Bring him back.

GEORGE

What?!

BUGSY

Hurry up.

As George chases after Mickey, Bugsy talks on the phone.

BUGSY

Jack?...Ben. Look, I think I've got the Mickey Cohen thing under control... Be at my house at seven-thirty tonight.

As Bugsy talks on the phone, he puts the cucumbers back on his eyes. After he hangs up he sits back and turns the sun lamp back on.

BUGSY

Twenty dwarves took turns doing handstands on the carpet.
Twenty dwarves took turns doing handstands on the carpet.

INT. BILTMORE BAR - DAY

Mickey and George are seated at a table in the bar. Bugsy walks in.

MICKEY

Hey, I know you're a big shot but make it quick, will you? I got a
hot date waitin' for me, and I don't have no time to be schmoozed
by the likes of you.

BUGSY

I'll bet you do.

MICKEY

I do what?

BUGSY

Have a hot date waiting for you.

MICKEY

You makin' fun of me?

BUGSY

Not at all. Guy with your balls must have more women lined up
than the Latin Quarter.

MICKEY

Whatever the fuck that's supposed to mean. I'll tell you one thing,
when I go out with a broad, you can bet she'll be a star. Like Betty
Grable or Ava Gardner. I don't go for them tarty broads like you
and your pal Joey A. go for.

BUGSY

What tarty broads?

MICKEY

Shirley what's-her-name, the broad that Charlie Luciano used to
drag around everywhere. That nutty broad Joey A.'s hung up on,
Victoria Hill. That six-foot giant bimbo Willy, that Gus and Moe
were seein' at the same time.

Bugsy meets with Mickey (left) and George in the Biltmore lounge

BUGSY

Virginia Hill.

MICKEY

Whatever.

BUGSY

(stung, but concealing it)

Why do you call her a tart?

MICKEY

'Cause that's what she is! Joe Epstein in Chicago, the bullfighters in Mexico — Gene Krupa, the drummer, the Frenchman — this conversation's beneath me.

BUGSY

(eagerly switching subjects)

Look, Mickey…I'm expanding. And I'm thinking — why should I expand with people who got taken? Why shouldn't I expand with the guy who took them?

MICKEY

What's in it for me?

BUGSY

Money.

MICKEY

How much?

BUGSY

Five thousand a week.

MICKEY

Does that include a blow job?

GEORGE

Watch your mouth, Mickey. This is Ben Siegel. You're lucky he don't plug you on the spot.

MICKEY

He can't. He needs me. He just said so. Ain't you been listenin'? Or have you been too busy learnin' lines for them fairy actin' jobs you're playin'?

BUGSY

Six.

MICKEY

Ten.

BUGSY

All right. Ten. But I want the forty-two thousand you stole back in my hands by seven o'clock tonight.

They start to shake hands but Mickey pulls back.

MICKEY

I put my life and liberty on the line for this fuckin' score. I'll kick back twenty. The whole forty-two — I wouldn't kick it back if you was my mother.

BUGSY

A penny less and we've got no deal.

Mickey stares at Bugsy. Finally he nods; walks off.

BUGSY

(to George)

How would Mickey know she fucked Gene Krupa and a bullfighter?

GEORGE

Well, it ain't exactly classified info, Baby Blue Eyes. Gene Krupa *I* know about…and a couple of the bullfighters.

BUGSY

A *couple* of the bullfighters?

GEORGE

Benny. Lookit. She is who she is. You ain't gonna change her. What man has ever changed a woman?

BUGSY

I don't go by what other people have done. I believe in fresh starts.

GEORGE

Fresh starts?

B U G S Y

Hey, without fresh starts, you and I would have been history
before we were nineteen.

INT. BUGSY'S HOUSE - DINING ROOM - NIGHT

Virginia comes in from the kitchen, puts down several dishes as Bugsy reads the *Los Angeles Times*
(accounts of Mussolini, Hitler, and the war). Virginia sits down.

V I R G I N I A

I hope you like shrimp scampi in a bed of soft brown rice rimmed
by carrots and peas.

B U G S Y

Uh-huh.

V I R G I N I A

What's wrong?

B U G S Y

Nothing.

V I R G I N I A

Come on. Eat. It'll make you big and strong.

B U G S Y

What do you think of bullfighting?

V I R G I N I A
(vaguely sensing what he's up to)
It's been a while since I tried it.

B U G S Y

What are your memories?

V I R G I N I A

Dangerous. And fun.

B U G S Y

What about drums?

V I R G I N I A

What *about* drums? I'm a singer.

BUGSY

You ever sing with a drummer?

VIRGINIA

I've sung with all kinds of musicians. Do you want to eat or not?
Dinner is getting cold.

BUGSY

It's already cold.

Virginia walks over to Bugsy, stands in front of him.

VIRGINIA

Were you under the impression that I was a virgin?

BUGSY

No. I just thought there might be somebody you *hadn't* fucked.

Virginia snatches a glass ashtray from the table and hurls it at Bugsy, hitting his head and opening
a cut, which bleeds down onto his face.

BUGSY

(pressing a hand to his wound)

Hey! That's not pleasant.

VIRGINIA

Listen to me, mister! You've fucked around and I've fucked
around. You want to tell me your stories? Fine! Then I'll tell you
mine. You want to bury the past where it belongs, we can do that
too. But don't try playing these sulky little games with me. I'll *kill*
you before I let you do that. What we share should be goddamn
good enough. And if it isn't, we should call it quits right here.
What'll it be?

BUGSY

How about some iodine?

VIRGINIA

You don't need iodine. You need soap and water. And wash your
fucking mouth out while you're at it. I'm going home.

She heads to the door. Bugsy pursues her, stops her.

BUGSY

Wait a second.

VIRGINIA

Let go of my arm.

The bell to the front door rings. Bugsy, still holding onto a resistant Virginia, opens the door with his other hand as blood pours down his face. It is Mickey.

MICKEY

Hey, Ben. You okay?

BUGSY

I'm fine.

Mickey hands Bugsy the cash.

MICKEY

Forty-two thousand even. On the nose.

BUGSY

Thank you. This is Virginia Hill.

MICKEY

Pleased to make your acquaintance. I've heard a lot about you.
(to Bugsy)
You want me to come in?

BUGSY

Would you be offended if I took a rain check?

MICKEY

Not under the circumstances. What happened to your head?

BUGSY

Vicious insect. I'll talk to you in the morning.

Mickey tips his panama hat and Bugsy closes the door.

EXT. BUGSY'S HOUSE - NIGHT

As Mickey walks to his car, Jack Dragna pulls up and parks directly behind Mickey. Jack gets out of his car as Mickey gets into his. Mickey sees Jack, but Jack doesn't see Mickey. As he pulls away, Mickey slows up, calls out to Jack:

MICKEY

Hey, Goombah...Kiss my *tuchas*!

Jack turns back; squints at Mickey. Mickey smiles and drives off.

> **JACK**
> (under his breath)

Fuck you, you Jew prick.

EXT. BUGSY'S HOUSE - NIGHT

We—and Jack—hear Bugsy and Virginia yelling at each other inside as Jack rings several times. Finally, Bugsy opens the door. His head is still bleeding. Jack comes in.

INT. BUGSY'S HOUSE - LIVING ROOM - NIGHT

Jack looks around the living room.

> **JACK**

Some joint in here. What happened to your head?

> **BUGSY**

Vicious insect.

> **JACK**

Yeah?
> (he looks at Virginia and then at Bugsy)

You'll never guess who I just saw driving by.

> **BUGSY**

Mickey Cohen.

> **JACK**

How did you know that?

> **BUGSY**
> (to Virginia)

Did you ever meet Jack Dragna?

> **VIRGINIA**

No.

> **BUGSY**
> (almost to himself)

Good.
> (to Virginia)

I gotta spend ninety seconds alone with Jack. Will you wait for me?

VIRGINIA

What for?

BUGSY

Will you wait for me?...*Please*.

They share a look; Virginia doesn't yield, doesn't answer.

INT. BUGSY'S HOUSE - STUDY - NIGHT

Bugsy leads Jack to the study, opens the door, and ushers Jack in. Bugsy pulls out the forty-two thousand Mickey has just given him.

JACK

The cocksucking thief dished it back?

BUGSY

Uh-huh. Every cent.

JACK

No kidding! Well, I'll be a son of a bitch! Mind if I ask how you got him to go along?

BUGSY

We reached an accommodation. He gave me the money and I gave him a job.

JACK

What job?

BUGSY

Running the day-to-day mechanics of my operation.

JACK

That's my job.

BUGSY

It *was* your job. Now you're working for him.

JACK

I think I'm missing something.

BUGSY

You certainly are. Fourteen thousand dollars. And change. Fourteen thousand dollars that you stole from us after the forty-two that Mickey took.

JACK

Wait a minute.

Bugsy looks coldly at Jack, works into a rage.

BUGSY

Do you want to fuck me?

JACK

What?

BUGSY

It's a simple question. Do you want to fuck me?

JACK

Of course not.

BUGSY

You sure?

JACK

Of course I'm sure. What —

INT. BUGSY'S HOUSE - LIVING ROOM - NIGHT

Virginia listens through the wall.

INT. BUGSY'S HOUSE - STUDY - NIGHT

BUGSY

Do you want to rape me?

JACK

This is crazy.

BUGSY

Shut up and answer the question.

                              JACK

No. I—

                            BUGSY

Don't lie to me.

                              JACK

No.

                            BUGSY

I said don't lie to me. You stole from me. Stealing is a form of rape. You wanted to rape me and humiliate me!

                              JACK

No. I—

                            BUGSY

Did you think you could get away with it?

                              JACK

I—

                            BUGSY

Did you think you could steal money from me, from us, from Meyer Lansky and Charlie Luciano and me, that you could rape us and humiliate us *and get away with it*?

                              JACK

What?

                            BUGSY

Did you think you could get away with it or not?

                              JACK

No.

                            BUGSY

Don't lie to me.

                              JACK

I'm not lying.

BUGSY

You're not lying? That means you raped us even though you thought we *would* catch you.

JACK

No. It wasn't like that.

BUGSY

What was it like?

JACK

I —

BUGSY

Shut up. You want to change your answer? It's a simple question. Did you think you would get away with it or not?

JACK

I —

BUGSY

Did you or not? Did you or not?

JACK

I'll never do it again. I promise.

BUGSY

You'll never *what*? You'll never do it *again*? What makes you think I won't kill you right here in this room?

Bugsy pulls his gun out of the desk drawer.

JACK

I beg you, Ben. Don't do it.

BUGSY

You wanna kill me? You want another chance?

Bugsy puts one bullet in the gun as he crosses around the desk. He offers the gun to Jack who refuses to take it.

BUGSY

You can't kill me. No one can kill me. *I* can't kill me.

Bugsy opens the barrel, removes five bullets so that only one remains; twirls the barrel around without looking at it, locks it back in, pushes it against his own temple, squeezes the trigger. A click is heard.

> **BUGSY**
>
> See?

Bugsy opens the barrel, twirls it again. Closes it and hands it to Jack.

> **BUGSY**
>
> You want to try it? Go ahead. Go ahead! Try it! Try it!

> **JACK**
>
> I can't. I—

> **BUGSY**
>
> Can't? Why not? You afraid to die?…Crawl!

> **JACK**
>
> What?

Suddenly, Bugsy grabs Jack by the ear, hurls him to the ground violently. He speaks in a frenzy.

> **BUGSY**
>
> Crawl around this room and bark like the dog you *wish* you were decent enough to be.

> **JACK**
>
> Look, I—

> **BUGSY**
>
> (with quiet, psychotic rage)
>
> Do it.

> **JACK**
>
> Bow-wow! Bow-wow! Bow-wow! Woof. Woof-woof. Woof.

INT. BUGSY'S HOUSE - LIVING ROOM - NIGHT

Virginia listens.

INT. BUGSY'S HOUSE - STUDY - NIGHT

BUGSY

Stay down there. Crawl around the other way and oink like the treacherous, devious pig you are.

JACK

I can't. I —

BUGSY

Do it!

Jack crawls.

INT. BUGSY'S HOUSE - LIVING ROOM - NIGHT

Virginia, even more puzzled, as she hears...

JACK
(V.O.)
Oink. Oink. Oink. Oink. Oink-oink. Oink.

INT. BUGSY'S HOUSE - STUDY - NIGHT

His crawling finished, Jack looks up at Bugsy who is now barely controlling his fury.

BUGSY

Stand up.

Jack stands; doesn't know what to do.

BUGSY

Now go home, get the money you stole and bring it to me.

He hands the forty-two thousand dollars Mickey gave him to Jack.

BUGSY

This money goes back into the safe in the betting parlor.

JACK

Thank you, Ben. You can count on me for anything.

BUGSY

(with an odd half-smile)
Yeah? We'll see. Everybody needs a fresh start once in a while.

Bugsy—bloodied by Virginia's hurled ashtray—confronts Jack Dragna.

INT. BUGSY'S HOUSE - LIVING ROOM - NIGHT

Bugsy comes out of the study behind Jack, walks him to the front door, and shows him out. Then he heads toward the dining room. He passes Virginia on the way.

Bugsy sits down at the dining room table and starts to eat savagely. Virginia follows him in and starts to kiss him. At first Bugsy continues to eat. Finally, he abandons his food, grabs Virginia, and they fall to the floor and make love.

EXT. BUGSY'S HOUSE - NIGHT

The lights are out.

INT. BUGSY'S HOUSE - BEDROOM - NIGHT

Virginia lies on top of Bugsy. Both are asleep and half-clothed. Virginia wakes up, looks at Bugsy as if he were a stranger. Bugsy awakens.

> **BUGSY**
>
> What is it?

Virginia looks at him without answering. She reaches over to turn on the light.

EXT. MULHOLLAND DRIVE - NIGHT

A vast sea of lights below as Bugsy and Virginia walk on Mulholland Drive.

> **VIRGINIA**
>
> Would you tell me if you were with someone else?

> **BUGSY**
>
> No...yes...no. What do you mean? I wouldn't be with someone...

> **VIRGINIA**
>
> Come on! Just answer me straight.

> **BUGSY**
>
> I would tell you the truth...I wouldn't keep a secret.

> **VIRGINIA**
>
> Who is the Countess Di Frasso?

B U G S Y

The Countess Di Frasso? Who is she? You're asking me?

V I R G I N I A

Yes, I'm asking you. Who is she?

B U G S Y

She's the wife of that Italian count. The Count Di Frasso. I danced with her at Ciro's.

V I R G I N I A

I *know* you "danced" with her.

B U G S Y

(conspiratorially)

Look, it just so happens the countess's husband, the count, is best friends with Mussolini.

V I R G I N I A

(looking at him blankly)

So?

B U G S Y

(with emphasis)

The countess's husband is Mussolini's best friend.

V I R G I N I A

I got it the first time. So what?

B U G S Y

The whole world is being destroyed by Hitler and Mussolini. I can do something about Mussolini.

V I R G I N I A

Do something about Mussolini?

B U G S Y

Yeah. Stop him.

V I R G I N I A

What do you mean, stop him?

BUGSY

What do you think I mean?

VIRGINIA

Kill him? *Kill Mussolini?*

BUGSY

Shhh…I'm going to use the count to get to Mussolini.

VIRGINIA

You're going to kill Mussolini personally in the middle of a war? That is the most pathetic, asinine, ludicrous excuse I've ever heard. If you want to fuck some lowlife countess, have the guts to *say* it. And then go ahead and do it—and why don't you kill yourself while you're at it.

BUGSY

You don't understand, sugar. I'm hatching a plan. A secret plan.

VIRGINIA

Yeah. You're full of secrets, aren't you?

BUGSY

What do you mean, secrets?

VIRGINIA

Secrets. Things that are not out in the open.

BUGSY

What's not out in the open?

VIRGINIA

Me.

BUGSY

You?

VIRGINIA

You're afraid to be seen with me. I'm a fucking secret.

BUGSY

From?

VIRGINIA

You know damn well! You told me you don't keep secrets from Esta.

BUGSY

Esta? That's different.

VIRGINIA

I know it's different. Because I'm just a secret—from *her*. And that's not what I want. I don't want to be anybody's secret from now on.

BUGSY

You're nobody's secret. Give me a chance.

VIRGINIA

You had your chance. We never go anywhere.

BUGSY

All right. From now on we go *everywhere*!

VIRGINIA

Everywhere?

BUGSY

Everywhere. Give me a chance. Everybody needs a fresh start once in a while.

EXT. SANTA MONICA AIRPORT - DAY

Bugsy, Mickey, and Virginia head toward a small plane. The engine is running. Suddenly Virginia stops. Bugsy turns back.

BUGSY

Come on, sugar.

VIRGINIA

I can't, Ben.

BUGSY

What's the matter?

VIRGINIA

I can't.

Virginia falls on her knees to keep Bugsy from pulling her.

VIRGINIA

You don't understand. I...I...I'm sorry. I thought I could but I can't.

BUGSY

Can't what?

VIRGINIA

Do it. I can't do it. I...Now that I see it...I can't. You have to understand.

BUGSY

Understand what?

VIRGINIA

I never have.

BUGSY

You never have what?

VIRGINIA

Been on a plane.

BUGSY

So?

VIRGINIA

Just go without me. It's ridiculous. I can't control you. I can't be with you every second. You're going to do whatever you're going to do. I can't be a watchdog.

BUGSY

A watchdog? What are you, crazy?

MICKEY

Ben! Come on. Let's go. The plane'll run out of gas.

BUGSY

Give me a second.

VIRGINIA

I'm not going.

BUGSY

I've seen this before. When I explain to you the basic rules of aerodynamics, you'll be just fine.

VIRGINIA

It won't make any difference. I'm not going.

INT. BUGSY'S CADILLAC - DAY

Bugsy is driving with Mickey in the passenger seat and Virginia in the back.

VIRGINIA

This is the most boring drive I've been on in my entire life.

BUGSY

If we'd *flown*, we'd have been there three hours ago.

VIRGINIA

I'm sorry. I should have just let you go alone. I don't even know why I came.

BUGSY

I don't even know why *I* came.
(to Mickey)

Why did I come?

MICKEY

You had to. You can't run an operation in Nevada and never go to Nevada.

EXT. LAS VEGAS CASINO (SHACK) - DAY

Bugsy, Mickey, and Virginia stand in front of a glorified shack billed as a "casino." They go inside.

INT. LAS VEGAS CASINO (SHACK) - DAY

Utter shabbiness: a couple of card tables, a few slot machines, a counter that passes for a bar, a tired bartender with five customers and two employees. Mickey seems to think it's fine. Bugsy looks around. Virginia is appalled.

VIRGINIA

(to Bugsy)

We drove five and a half hours for *this*?…This *canker* sore?

MICKEY

It may not look it, but there's a steady profit comin' out of this here joint. It's got regular customers with nowhere else to spend their money.

VIRGINIA

I'd get rid of it.

MICKEY

We got everything to gain and nothing to lose. The upkeep's almost zero.

VIRGINIA

Who would have thought? It looks as if a fortune were spent in here every day.

MICKEY

That's not the point. Looks don't matter when there's money comin' in.

VIRGINIA

Looks matter if it matters how you look. Personally, I think the place should be boarded up and burned.

MICKEY

I wouldn't go that far, Victoria.

BUGSY

Victoria? Her name is *Virginia*! Find the manager.

MICKEY

(to Virginia)

I didn't call you Victoria, did I?

VIRGINIA

Yes, you did.

BUGSY

Will you get the manager, please?

Mickey goes to get the manager.

INT. BUGSY'S CAR - DAY

Bugsy drives, with Mickey asleep in the passenger seat and Virginia in the back.

> **BUGSY**
>
> Don't ever embarrass me that way again in front of my associates.

> **VIRGINIA**
>
> I was right.

> **BUGSY**
>
> No, Mickey was right. The place made money. It should have stayed open.

> **VIRGINIA**
>
> Then why did you close it?

> **BUGSY**
>
> Because you were right too. It *was* a canker sore. But you made me look as if I were your fucking puppet.

> **VIRGINIA**
>
> Maybe you *need* someone to tell you what to do — even if it isn't what you want to hear. But maybe you're not up to that. Maybe you just want to continue dodging and lying your way through two lives, checking at home in Scarsdale for reassurance whenever you get too lonely. Maybe you're getting too old.

Bugsy slams on the brakes, waking Mickey.

> **BUGSY**
>
> I take too much from you. And it's gonna stop right now.

> **VIRGINIA**
>
> Hot air in a hot desert.

> **BUGSY**
>
> You don't talk to me about Scarsdale. Scarsdale's none of your business.

Bugsy gives her a look and gets out. He strides into the desert, paces around, and then stops suddenly, as if struck by an epiphany. He gestures inventively.

VIRGINIA

What is he doing?

MICKEY

Looking for a place to take a leak, I guess.

Virginia looks at Mickey as if he were crazier than Bugsy. Mickey gets out of the car. Bugsy, satisfied that he has solved spatial problems and ordered his revelations, rushes back to the car with the good news. Virginia slips into the driver's seat.

BUGSY

I got it! I got it!

MICKEY

What?

BUGSY

It came to me like a vision. Like a religious epiphany.

MICKEY

You're not talkin' about God, are you, Ben?

BUGSY

No. I am talking about the single greatest idea I ever had.

VIRGINIA

Yeah? Well, I have the single greatest idea I ever had.

She drives away.

MICKEY

Oy-oy-oy-oy-oy!

BUGSY

Isn't she magnificent?

MICKEY

Yeah. Just what I've always been looking for — a broad who'll leave me alone in the middle of a desert to drop dead and be eaten by vultures…So what's this idea of yours?

BUGSY

I can't say yet, Mickey. I've got to get it in motion first.

MICKEY

I think you got problems, Ben. I think she's got divorce on the brain.

Bugsy and Mickey continue walking down the highway.

INT. HOLLYWOOD - CIRO'S - NIGHT

Dissolve from the blistering sun of the desert to the spotlight on stage, revealing a SINGER doing a rendition of "Long Ago and Far Away."

EXT. HOLLYWOOD - CIRO'S - NIGHT

An elegant crowd flows in and out of the nightclub and we see Virginia arrive in the silver Cadillac convertible driven by her date, ALEJANDRO.

INT. HOLLYWOOD - CIRO'S - NIGHT

Bugsy sits at a corner table with Dorothy, having caviar and Dom Perignon. Dorothy is already tipsy.

DOROTHY

Yes, but Benjy dear, what would we *do* in Italy with all those bullets flying around?

BUGSY

Meet Mussolini.

DOROTHY

You *are* outrageous! Of course, that's what I love about you.

Bugsy pours Dorothy another glass of champagne.

DOROTHY

But *why* do you want to meet the Duce?

BUGSY

I have friends in Naples who could use his help. Now, can your husband arange a meeting with Mussolini or do people exaggerate his connections?

DOROTHY
(moving her lips to within an inch of Bugsy's)
My husband can get you this close to the Duce whenever he wishes and he will wish to do whatever I say.

As Dorothy continues, Bugsy sees Virginia and Alejandro being seated by the maitre d'; Bugsy's attention and rising jealous anger are focused on them. Virginia notices Bugsy, too, but then, instead of looking back, concentrates on Alejandro.

DOROTHY

I'm a very intuitive person, Benjamin. And you know what my intuition tells me about you? That you always get exactly what you want. Don't deny it! I find your confidence irresistible. I find myself…sucked in by it… helpless, if you must know the truth.

Bugsy is going crazy over Virginia. He gets up.

BUGSY

(to Dorothy with his eyes on Virginia)

Excuse me.

Bugsy walks over to Virginia and Alejandro.

With plans for an assassination, Bugsy cajoles an introduction to Mussolini from Dorothy di Frasso

BUGSY

There are a few little wrinkles to iron out, but it looks as if that secret plan I was telling you about is going through.

(Virginia doesn't react)

I'm leaving for New York tomorrow, so I thought I'd come over to say hello and good-bye.

VIRGINIA

(coolly)

Hello and good-bye.

BUGSY

I've got some problems there. You know Charlie was arrested…My old friend Harry Greenberg must have testified against him…and, uh…

VIRGINIA

Am I supposed to be interested in this?

Alejandro laughs.

BUGSY

What does your friend do for a living? Stick knives into helpless animals?

VIRGINIA

He's a guitarist.

(pointing to Alejandro)

Flamenco.

(pointing to herself)

Flamingo.

BUGSY

You're not actually going to spend the night with this creep, are you?

Alejandro jumps to his feet.

ALEJANDRO

I demand a retraction.

VIRGINIA

What I do with my time and my body is my business. Sit down, Alejandro.

A L E J A N D R O

I demand satisfaction.

Bugsy pulls out a .38, concealing it from all but Virginia and Alejandro, at whom he points it.

B U G S Y

Would this satisfy you, sweetie?

Alejandro twitches.

V I R G I N I A
(to Bugsy)
Take a hike, will you. Go back to your cuntess, you hypocritical son of a bitch. I hope she gives you syphilis.
(to Alejandro)
Let's get out of this joint, Alejandro.

As she and Alejandro get up, Bugsy speaks.

B U G S Y

I'm going to be asking Esta for a divorce.

V I R G I N I A

You better get to a phone.

B U G S Y

I'm going to do it in New York.

V I R G I N I A
(still reacting coolly)

Good luck.

She storms away with Alejandro in tow.

EXT. UNION STATION - ESTABLISHING SHOT

INT. UNION STATION - COFFEE SHOP - DAY

A tight shot of the headline of the *Examiner* which reads "BUGSY SIEGEL SCANDAL AT CIRO'S" (The subheading next to a sinister photograph of Bugsy, reads: "Notorious Gangster's Death Threat His Latest Outrage." The camera pulls back and reveals Bugsy ranting as he reads the article while Mickey reads (lip syncing all the way) a report in the *Los Angeles Times*.

BUGSY

I was wearing a *blue silk* shirt? I don't even *own* a blue silk shirt. I was "brandishing" a forty-five "menacingly." What an outrageous fabrication! It wasn't a forty-five at all. It was a thirty-eight. And I wasn't brandishing it. I was *concealing* it — subtly — to make a point....What kind of vile, despicable people write these lies?

MICKEY

(absently)

I agree with you a hundred percent. They got no morals, those people...

(focusing on the article he is reading)

Benny, everything we heard last night is true. Charlie's in jail because of this rat-bastard stool pigeon, Harry Greenberg.... Don't you *know* this guy Harry Greenberg?

Mickey shoves a page-eight article in front of Bugsy. It has a large photograph of Harry Greenberg next to a photo of Charlie. The headline reads: "MOB HUNTS UN-'LUCKY'S' STOOL PIGEON." The subheadline reads: "Big Greenie Canary Sings Charlie Into His Cage." The caption under Harry's picture reads: "Harry 'Big Greenie' Greenberg"; the caption under Charlie's picture reads: "Charlie 'Lucky' Luciano."

BUGSY

(stricken)

Yeah. I know him...I'm getting a divorce, Mickey.

MICKEY

I'm sorry to hear that.

BUGSY

I have no choice. I'm going to New York, and I'm getting a divorce.

EXT. SCARSDALE - BUGSY'S HOUSE - NIGHT

The lights are on inside Bugsy's house. A black Cadillac pulls up. Meyer, Frank, Joey A., Vito, Gus, and Moe get out and head toward the front door.

INT. BUGSY'S SCARSDALE HOUSE - DINING ROOM - KITCHEN - NIGHT

The main courses of dinner are over. Millicent leans to see Bugsy (in an apron and chef's hat), Esta, and Barbara through a partially closed kitchen door. Bugsy is putting the finishing decorative touches on an elaborate chocolate birthday cake. He is writing the words "Happy Birthday Millicent — 9" in pink icing. (Esta is pouring glasses of milk and fixing coffee. Barbara is collecting dishes, silverware, and napkins.) Colorful gas balloons press against the kitchen ceiling.

Bugsy tries to explain to his daughter Millicent (Stephanie Mason) why he must interrupt her birthday party to take care of business…

M I L L I C E N T

I know what you're doing!

B U G S Y

No, you don't. And don't take one step further until we're done in here.

M I L L I C E N T

I do too know. You're writing "Happy Birthday, Millicent" on my birthday cake.

Bugsy looks at Esta, who smiles.

B U G S Y

(to Barbara)

Set the table, honey, will you?

B A R B A R A

Okay.

Barbara starts out. Bugsy has an afterthought, stops her; whispers.

B U G S Y

Where'd you hide our presents?

B A R B A R A

They're with the potatoes.

Barbara goes to a drawer, opens it and reveals a bunch of gift-wrapped boxes.

B U G S Y

The presents are with the potatoes?

Barbara giggles. Bugsy shakes his head. Barbara takes the place settings into the dining room. Esta puts the milk and coffee on a tray. There is a double ring of the front doorbell.

E S T A

(unpleasantly surprised)

Who could *that* be?

B U G S Y

Don't move. I'll be right back.

Bugsy runs out.

INT. BUGSY'S SCARSDALE HOUSE - FRONT HALLWAY - NIGHT

Bugsy runs through the dining room.

BUGSY

Barbara, get rid of the thing in the middle.

Bugsy opens the front door. Meyer stands in front of Joey A., Frank, Vito, and Moe, who appears to be Meyer's attendant. Bugsy keeps his chef's hat and apron on throughout.

MEYER

I hope we're not disturbing you, Ben.

BUGSY

Not at all. We were just wrapping up a little birthday party for Millicent.

MEYER

There's an urgent matter we have to discuss.

BUGSY

Good, because I have an urgent matter to discuss with you. Come on in.

There is a tense, silent moment between Bugsy and Joey A. as the men walk in.

BUGSY

Make yourselves at home. Pour yourselves a drink.

INT. BUGSY'S SCARSDALE HOUSE - DINING ROOM - NIGHT

Bugsy rushes back through the dining room, holding his finger in the air as if to say "one more second."

INT. BUGSY'S SCARSDALE HOUSE - KITCHEN - NIGHT

Bugsy enters the kitchen where Esta is still holding the tray.

BUGSY

(to Esta, as if he expects her to be pleased)
Guess who that is! Meyer, Joey A., Frank, Vito, and Moe!

ESTA

I thought maybe we would have this one night to ourselves?

BUGSY

I'm sorry, Esta. I was planning on seeing them tomorrow.

ESTA

Does Meyer know it's Millicent's birthday?

BUGSY

I told them, but I think they've got a little problem with a business thing I did. Let me just put it to rest. Can you finish the writing on the cake and put the candles on? I'll be right back.

Bugsy rushes out.

INT. BUGSY'S SCARSDALE HOUSE - DEN - NIGHT

Bugsy rushes into the den. The five visitors are waiting, seated stonily.

BUGSY

Before I get to what's important, I have to tell you guys that I got rid of that seedy little canker sore of a shack in Las Vegas which was the center of our operations there.

MEYER

That's what we came to talk to you about, Ben. You had no *right* to give that casino up.

BUGSY

Casino…It was an outhouse.

MEYER

It made a profit every month. You had no right to close it without consulting us.

VITO

That's the arrangement we got, ain't it?

BUGSY

(to Vito)

Arrangement? I don't have any "arrangment" with you, Vito. I have an arrangement with Meyer and Charlie, but don't worry.

…when Meyer Lansky (Ben Kingsley, foreground) and associates Vito Genovese (Don Carrara, left), Moe Sedway (Joe Romano, center), Frank Costello (Carmine Caridi, second right), and Gus Greenbaum (James Toback, right), show up unexpectedly at Bugsy's Scarsdale home…

…and Millicent's birthday celebration is put on hold as Bugsy welcomes his guests: Gus Greenbaum (seated), Meyer Lansky, Frank Costello (background), and Joey Adonis (right)

Meyer and Joey A. listen to what Bugsy is proposing

When I tell you what I'm going to build in place of that rancid little toilet bowl, you'll understand for the first time the meaning of the word *transcendent*!

MEYER

Tell us now.

BUGSY

I found the answer to the dreams of America.

MEYER

Could you be a little more specific?

BUGSY

The Flamingo!

FRANK

A bird?

BUGSY

Let me ask you, what are people always having fantasies about? Sex, romance, money, and adventure. I'm building a monument to all of them.

VITO

What are you talking about here? A whorehouse?

BUGSY

I'm talking about a hotel. I'm talking about *Las Vegas*, *Nevada*. I'm talking about a place where gambling is allowed, where *everything* is allowed. The whole *territory* is wide open. I'm talking about a palace, an *oasis*…a city. Do you realize when the Hoover Dam is finished, electrical power will be available on a massive scale in Las Vegas?

FRANK

I don't follow. The Hoover Dam and fucking are connected *how*?

BUGSY

By air conditioning! It's the wave of the future. Everything will be cooled. Every room will be seventy-two degrees at all times. The casino will put Monte Carlo to shame—with Italian marble and wall-to-wall carpeting! And badminton courts and stables. There'll be lightning-fast trains—Los Angeles to Las Vegas in an hour. And planes! Back and forth. Meyer, we'll have our own airport!

M E Y E R

(to Frank)

I think what Ben is saying is… it's a good place to trap people in to take their money.

(to Ben)

Is that what you're getting at here, Benny.?

B U G S Y

Much more. Much, much more.

The group looks bewildered. The phone rings. As Bugsy runs out, he yells to Esta.

B U G S Y

I got it! I got it!

INT. BUGSY'S SCARSDALE HOUSE - HALLWAY TABLE - NIGHT

As the phone continues to ring, Bugsy grabs it and whispers into it conspiratorially.

B U G S Y

Hello…Mickey! Have you got someone parked across the street from her house?…Call Ciro's and call Warner's now and see if anybody's seen her. Call me right back…No. Not *five* minutes— *one* minute!

Bugsy hangs up.

INT. BUGSY'S SCARSDALE HOUSE - DINING ROOM - NIGHT

As Bugsy — his index finger pointed up in the air to ask for one more second — rushes by Millicent, who is sitting alone at the dining room table, and into the kitchen, he speaks.

B U G S Y

(to Millicent)

Let me see how they're doing.

INT. BUGSY'S SCARSDALE HOUSE - KITCHEN - DINING ROOM - NIGHT

Bugsy finds Esta and Barbara in the kitchen.

B U G S Y

Everything moving along?…Hey, that looks great! (to Barbara) Your mother's a real artist, did you know that? I'm gonna run back in there. I think I got these guys going on this thing.

E S T A

Ben. Don't keep the girls waiting too long. Children don't have the patience adults do.

B U G S Y

I know that. That's what I'm saying. You do the candles in here and I'll finish up in there and then we'll both be ready!

He runs out, passes Millicent in the dining room on his way to the den.

B U G S Y

Don't move an inch, my little birthday girl.

INT. BUGSY'S SCARSDALE HOUSE - DEN - NIGHT

Bugsy returns.

M E Y E R

Ben. I don't understand this desert thing of yours. What are we, Bedouins? What's wrong with concentrating on Cuba? You've got legalized gambling down there too, and you're right off the coast of Florida. It's like another state.

B U G S Y

Like another state, but *not* another state. A foreign country can always throw you out. Nevada *is* another state. It's open. If we do this right, follow the hotel with a church, a synagogue, schools...build all the things that give a city backbone, we'll be in *charge* before you know it.

M E Y E R

In charge of what?

B U G S Y

The state! And if you've got a state, the whole *country* is within your reach.

J O E Y A .

You plannin' to run for President?

B U G S Y

No reason we can't help to *choose* the President if we control the state. Why be bogged down by petty limitations? Open your eyes to the horizon.

The phone rings. Bugsy jumps up.

BUGSY

I got it! I got it!

MEYER

Can't anybody else get the phone?

INT. BUGSY'S SCARSDALE HOUSE - HALLWAY TABLE - NIGHT

Bugsy picks up the phone.

BUGSY

Hello?…Do you mean to tell me that I have you and sixty-five guys under you on my payroll and nobody can find Virginia?…Mickey. Listen to me carefully. I cannot function effectively when I'm in a state of ignorance. Find her.

Bugsy hangs up.

INT. BUGSY'S SCARSDALE HOUSE - KITCHEN - NIGHT

Bugsy stops next to Millicent.

BUGSY

Hold the fort. Daddy will be with you in a couple of minutes… What's wrong?

MILLICENT

I thought you came home because you wanted to be with me on my birthday.

BUGSY

I did. I *am* with you. I just — I have this meeting to finish up — and then —

MILLICENT

Daddy, you always say that. I don't want to talk to you.

Millicent starts to cry, runs through the service area, up the back staircase. Bugsy rushes after her.

BUGSY

Millicent! Wait! Honey, come back.

Millicent ignores him, runs upstairs into her room and slams the door behind her. Bugsy turns to Esta who has come from the kitchen to the edge of the dining room.

> **BUGSY**
>
> Are you going to let her just run away like that?

> **ESTA**
>
> Am *I* going to? Why don't you leave with your friends and come back when you're through? It would be better for everyone.

> **BUGSY**
>
> Wait a minute. I think I may be convincing these guys to go forward with one of the most ambitious projects we've ever been involved with.

Bugsy turns to Barbara.

> **BUGSY**
>
> Barb. Run upstairs and tell your sister to come down.
> (Barbara shakes her head no)
> I'll make you a deal. Get Millicent to come down out of her room and I'll get rid of all my friends.
> (Barbara goes upstairs; Bugsy continues to Esta)
> Light the candles and I'll be right back.

Bugsy runs out.

INT. BUGSY'S SCARSDALE HOUSE - DEN - NIGHT

Bugsy runs from the outer hallway, through the foyer into the den.

As Bugsy comes in, Meyer speaks.

> **MEYER**
>
> If you want to meet, let's have a meeting.

> **BUGSY**
>
> Of course.

> **MEYER**
>
> Vito?

> **VITO**
>
> Where do you think the money for this...

JOEY A.

Palace…

VITO

…is gonna come from?

BUGSY

Well, since I'll be doing all the work, but the partners will be
sharing in the success, the money should come from them.

VITO

"Them" meaning who?

BUGSY

"Them" meaning you.

MEYER

How much are we talking about, Ben?

BUGSY

A million dollars.

MEYER

What about the publicity? A place like this will cause a lot of talk.
The spotlight will be on us every day.

JOEY A.

Ben is gettin' famous out in California.

MEYER

Famous isn't good, Ben. For Clark Gable it's good. For Joe
DiMaggio it's good. Famous for you isn't good.

BUGSY

(firmly and decisively)

The Flamingo will make all our gambling interests legitimate.
Meyer. Listen. We've known each other since we were too young to
fuck. Did I ever ask you to close your eyes, shut off that thinking
of yours and just leap into something on faith? Never! But I'm
asking you now. Do this.

Bugsy raises his finger for silence and listens.

BUGSY

Did anyone hear the phone?

As Bugsy runs out, the rest of the group looks at each other in growing dismay.

INT. BUGSY'S SCARSDALE HOUSE - HALLWAY TABLE - NIGHT

Bugsy rushes in and picks up the phone.

> **BUGSY**
>
> Hello?…Hello?

He hangs up.

INT. BUGSY'S SCARSDALE - DINING ROOM/STAIRCASE - HALLWAY -NIGHT

Bugsy sees Esta sitting alone, head in hands at the dining room table.

> **ESTA**
>
> Ben…

> **BUGSY**
>
> No one lit the candles? Where's Barbara? Where's Barbara?

> **ESTA**
>
> Upstairs with her sister.

> **BUGSY**
>
> I thought she was going to bring her down. What's going on around here? What's all the bedlam?

INT. BUGSY'S HOUSE - UPSTAIRS HALLWAY - NIGHT

Bugsy runs upstairs and knocks on his daughters' bedroom door.

> **BUGSY**
>
> Millicent!…Open the door, honey…I just want to say one thing, okay?…Barbara?…Are you in there, too? Why don't you both come down so we can have the party?

> **BARBARA**
> (OS)
>
> Are the men gone yet?

> **BUGSY**
>
> They have one foot out the door. They'll be gone in — Just come down. I'm gonna light the candles.

He knocks again. There is no response. Bugsy runs downstairs.

> **BUGSY**
>
> I'm gonna light the candles. You better come down. I'm lighting the candles.

INT. BUGSY'S SCARSDALE HOUSE - DOWNSTAIRS HALLWAY - NIGHT

Bugsy is intercepted by Meyer on his way to Esta.

> **MEYER**
>
> Ben.

> **BUGSY**
>
> Don't worry. The party got a little out of control but I fixed it.

> **MEYER**
>
> Charlie's in Dannemora penitentiary. I'll have to confer with him to make any important money decision final. Pending that talk and his approval, I'm ready to say you've got yourself a deal.

> **BUGSY**
>
> Good. Good. Great.

> **MEYER**
>
> When would you be ready to get started?

> **BUGSY**
>
> As soon as I get back from Italy. I'm leaving in one week — that plus however long it takes.

> **MEYER**
>
> However long what takes?

> **BUGSY**
> (sotto voce)
>
> The assassination of Mussolini.

> **MEYER**
>
> Who's going to assassinate Mussolini?

Bugsy gives Meyer a look which says: "Who beside me could do it?"

MEYER

(with a forced smile, motioning to Bugsy)

Come here.

(he leads Bugsy farther away from the others)

Lookit, Benny. Don't fuck it up by trying to be funny.

BUGSY

I'm not being funny. Mussolini and Hitler have to be stopped. They're trying to knock off every Jew on earth. If *I* don't do something about it, who will? A bunch of Italians?

(indicating the others)

I can stop Mussolini.

MEYER

Did you ever hear of the Allied Forces? Why don't you leave it to them?

BUGSY

You're missing the point. The Allied Forces don't have the access. I have the access.

MEYER

You have the access.

Bugsy looks around; no one is near. Meyer waits.

BUGSY

One of Mussolini's best friends is the Count di Frasso. The Count di Frasso's wife, Dorothy, has the hots for me and she'll get me right up close to this cocksucker Mussolini so I can blow him halfway to Siberia.

MEYER

Ben. Listen to me very carefully. Don't ever repeat what you just said to me to anybody else.

BUGSY

That's right. Keep it secret.

MEYER

I'm saying it to you for a different reason.

BUGSY

Why are you saying it to me?

MEYER

Because at best...*at best*...any normal person you say it to would never take anything you say seriously again. So nothing more to the guys. Okay?

BUGSY

Sure. But Mussolini is a dead man.
(Meyer looks at Bugsy)
I'll be with you in a minute.

Bugsy returns to the dining room. Meyer goes back to the gang.

INT. BUGSY'S SCARSDALE HOUSE - DINING ROOM/KITCHEN - NIGHT

Bugsy runs into the kitchen and we hear his voice.

BUGSY

(yelling out)
I'm lighting the candles!...I'm lighting the candles!

Bugsy emerges from the kitchen into the service area carrying the cake with lighted candles.

BUGSY

(yelling out)
I lit the candles!...I lit the candles!

Bugsy walks through the service area and into the dining room, placing the cake in the middle of the table.

BUGSY

(yelling out)
I lit the candles!...I lit the candles!

Bugsy walks through the foyer, yelling upstairs to the girls' room. There is no response. Bugsy returns to the den.

BUGSY'S SCARSDALE HOUSE - DEN - NIGHT

Bugsy enters, addressing Meyer.

BUGSY

So! We finished with our other business?

MEYER

As far as I can see. We shouldn't have barged in on you like this.
Enjoy your party for little Millicent. We'll talk tomorrow.

(lower)

It sounds good.

Meyer motions to Frank, Vito, Gus, and Moe that it is time for them all to leave.

INT. BUGSY'S SCARSDALE HOUSE - FRONT DOOR - NIGHT

As they walk out, Meyer stops, kisses and hugs Ben. Then he leaves. There is a long moment of awkward silence between Bugsy and Joey A.

BUGSY

Listen, Joey, I'm sorry about Virginia. You want to punch me? Go
ahead and punch me.

Joey A. punches Bugsy cleanly through the jaw, knocking him on his back.

Bugsy, stunned, on the floor, massaging his jaw, moves to avoid being viewable from the dining room.

BUGSY

We're even now.

(low)

I'm sorry. I know you were in love with her.

JOEY A.

Are you kiddin' me? I was never in love with her. You think I'd let
myself fall in love with a slut like that?

BUGSY

You better get out of here, Joey.

Joey A., with a smirk of satisfaction, turns and leaves as Bugsy presses a handkerchief to his mouth to stop the blood.

INT. BUGSY'S SCARSDALE HOUSE - DINING ROOM - NIGHT

No one is in the room. The candles have burned down. Bugsy is seated. His mouth starts to bleed. Esta comes in, looks at Bugsy.

ESTA

Your mouth is bleeding.

BUGSY

Oh…I tripped and whacked it on the table. It's nothing.

He blots his mouth with a napkin.

ESTA

I don't think we can go on like this, Ben.

BUGSY

Like what?

ESTA

Do you think we should get a divorce?

BUGSY

What are you talking about? Some friends dropped by at the wrong time, that's all. Everything's *fine* now.

Esta is silent. Bugsy strains to seem oblivious.

EXT. LOS ANGELES - VIRGINIA'S HOUSE - DUSK

A taxi pulls up in front of Virginia's house.

INT. VIRGINIA'S HOUSE - LIVING ROOM - DUSK

Virginia opens the peephole in the door and sees Bugsy.

BUGSY

Did you miss me?

She closes the peephole and opens the door for Bugsy to enter.

VIRGINIA

You crossed my mind.

They walk through the living room and into the den.

BUGSY

We've got to celebrate. I sold them on the idea. I have it all worked out in my mind. I can see it in the most minute detail. We've got to drink a toast to our destiny.

INT. VIRGINIA'S HOUSE - DEN - BAR - NIGHT

VIRGINIA

So! Did you ask her for a divorce?

BUGSY

Not in so many words. But I've laid the groundwork so that
when —

VIRGINIA

Do me a favor. It's the only favor I'll ever ask of you.

BUGSY

Anything.

VIRGINIA

Finish your drink, get the fuck out of here, and never come near
me again.

BUGSY

Sugar, you don't understand. I was laying the groundwork…

At this point, Bugsy sees CHICK HILL in the adjacent room. He is reclining in a lounge chair in his silk bathrobe, with nothing on underneath. Bugsy, incensed beyond control, rushes over, and despite Virginia's screaming he grabs a stunned and terrified Chick by the lapels.

BUGSY

Having a good time?

Bugsy rips him up from his chair and hurls him through the French doors.

VIRGINIA

Ben! You maniac! You fucking lunatic! Look what you've done.

Virginia runs outside. Bugsy follows.

EXT. VIRGINIA'S HOUSE - SHRUBBERY - DUSK

Virginia rushes over to attend the battered Chick. Bugsy is furious that she cares.

VIRGINIA

(to Chick)
Are you okay, baby? Are you hurt?

Bugsy at the broken window through which he has just thrown Virginia Hill's brother, Chick, mistaking him for one of Virginia's suitors

Chick groans.

BUGSY

I don't know if you're hurt, but you're one lucky son of a bitch you're alive. I'll give you three minutes to get your little panties on and get the hell out of here.

VIRGINIA

He's my brother, you psychotic asshole!

BUGSY

You really expect me to fall for that?

VIRGINIA

I don't care what you fall for. I only care that you get psychiatric help, and that you never come around here bothering us anymore.

BUGSY

Us!

Bugsy is about to trounce Chick again, but Virginia grabs at him and shrieks.

VIRGINIA

Leave him alone! HE'S MY BROTHER!!

CHICK
(groggily)

I am! I am! I am!

BUGSY
(calmer)

Would you mind showing me some form of identification?

Lamely, Chick points to the adjacent room.

CHICK

It's in my pants in the guest bathroom.

As Virginia consoles Chick, Bugsy storms into the next room, finds Chick's pants, removes the wallet and examines the cards inside. He returns to Chick and Virginia.

BUGSY

You're right.
(to Chick)
You're *Chick*! You *are* her brother.

(to Virginia)

Why didn't you *tell* me he was *Chick*?

(turns to Chick)

I'm gonna buy you a Cadillac, Chick.

C H I C K

(buoyed)

A Cadillac?

B U G S Y

How's red? A convertible!

C H I C K

Wow! A red Cadillac convertible!

V I R G I N I A

Don't sell out so cheap.

Virginia storms off toward the stairs.

Virginia explains that Chick really is her brother

CHICK

That's not cheap. I've wanted a Cadillac since I was six years old.

Bugsy turns and follows her.

BUGSY

And you know what we're gonna do with Chick's new Cadillac?
We're going to take a trip —

They start up the stairs.

VIRGINIA

You're gonna take a trip.

BUGSY

(almost to himself)

To our destiny…Las Vegas.

VIRGINIA

Las Vegas! You couldn't drag me back into that sand trap, rat hole
with a fishnet!

Virginia reaches the top of the stairs, enters her room and slams the door.

INT. VIRGINIA'S HOUSE - BEDROOM - DUSK

Bugsy opens the door and follows her through the room.

BUGSY

Sugar, we're going to build a little Garden of Eden in the desert. A
hotel, but not a hotel.

Virginia walks into the dressing room and slams the door in Bugsy's face. Bugsy turns and walks
back through Virginia's room and into the hallway. She slams the door in Bugsy's face again.

BUGSY

A palace! An oasis with a casino.

Virginia walks through the dressing room to the door to the hallway.

VIRGINIA

You are insane.

Bugsy opens the door and follows her in.

> **BUGSY**
>
> It's all legal. It's Nevada.

Virginia walks into the bathroom and slams the door. Bugsy walks through the dressing room and back into the hallway.

> **BUGSY**
>
> We'll have palm trees and pools and flower gardens more lush than Versailles. And we'll design it all ourselves.

Virginia crosses through the bathroom, slams and locks the door to the hallway.

> **VIRGINIA**
>
> Get away from me.

Bugsy stays outside the door.

> **BUGSY**
>
> We're going to have the greatest entertainers in the world. Durante! Cantor! And Jolson! Ted Lewis! Sophie Tucker! Benny Goodman! Tommy Dorsey! The biggest stars from Hollywood'll come for days. Cary Grant! Gary Cooper! Dana Andrews! Victor Mature! They'll all be hanging around because it'll be the most spectacular place they've ever been invited to. And you're gonna own five and three quarters percent. That's gross, not net.

Virginia has sneaked back through her bedroom and is standing in the doorway, undetected, behind Bugsy.

> **BUGSY**
>
> We'll be the greatest hosts in the West. And you know what we're calling it? The Flamingo.

> **VIRGINIA**
>
> You know...
>
> (Bugsy turns to looks at Virginia)
>
> I've brought nothing but trouble to every man who ever went on the line for me.

> **BUGSY**
>
> Good. That's what they get for trying to steal my girl.

INT. BUGSY'S HOUSE - LIVING ROOM - DAY

Bugsy, Virginia (with a checkbook and sheets of financial records in front of her), Mickey, George, DEL WEBB, DAVID HINTON, Chick, and Moe examine floor plans, architectural sketches, miniature models, building designs, and various samples of material — all connected to the construction of the Flamingo. Bugsy — the first section of the *Examiner* in his hand — paces the room, alternately looking at the paper and eyeing Virginia and David.

V I R G I N I A

Sensational, David!

D A V I D

Well, thank you!

V I R G I N I A

(to Del — rhetorically)
Where'd you find this guy, Del? He's terrific.

G E O R G E

I must say — it looks gorgeous to me, Ben. Very European. Very French.

M I C K E Y

You could sell these here objects in a museum. This is not easy stuff to draw.

Bugsy looks at Virginia and at David.

B U G S Y

The relationship of the pool bothers me.

V I R G I N I A

What's wrong with the relationship of the pool?

B U G S Y

If you were paying attention you'd see there's not enough sun.

V I R G I N I A

But isn't —

B U G S Y

(interrupting her and ignoring her; to Del)
Del, I think your assistant's got to pay a little more attention. If we

slid the pool up to here, wouldn't it get more sun? Because then this part of the main building wouldn't shield it. Am I right or not?

DEL

I would think you are.

(to David)

David?

DAVID

Sure. But that would change the perspective of the pool in relation to the casino.

BUGSY

I'm only interested in one thing. If we move the pool, will the sun hit the pool all day — directly?

DAVID

Yes, it will.

BUGSY

Move the pool.

DEL

I hate to bear bad tidings but we have inflated the budget to two million by now.

BUGSY

No problem.

Simultaneously, Virginia, Mickey, George and Moe look incredulously at Bugsy.

MOE

I've gotta give Meyer a call.

MICKEY

That's a lot of extra money, Ben.

Bugsy, without missing a beat, turns, opens the newspaper and, muttering to himself, wanders off, staring at the front page — whose headline reads "MUSSOLINI MURDERED — Italians Butcher Brutal Dictator" and whose accompanying photograph shows Mussolini's corpse hanging upside down.

BUGSY

I can't believe he's dead. I just can't believe it.

Virginia at the construction site of the Flamingo Hotel in Las Vegas

M I C K E Y

How long are you gonna keep saying you can't believe it? He was dead the first time you picked up the paper, he's dead now, and he'll still be dead an hour from now.

B U G S Y

I was moments away from carrying out my plan. *Moments away.*

M I C K E Y

Ben. For Chrissakes, relax. The cocksucker's dead. That's what matters. And look at how they got him! You couldn't have done a better job yourself.

B U G S Y

(looking straight into Mickey's eyes)

I couldn't have?

Mickey turns to leave; Bugsy continues, his voice low.

Mickey Cohen on the site of the Flamingo

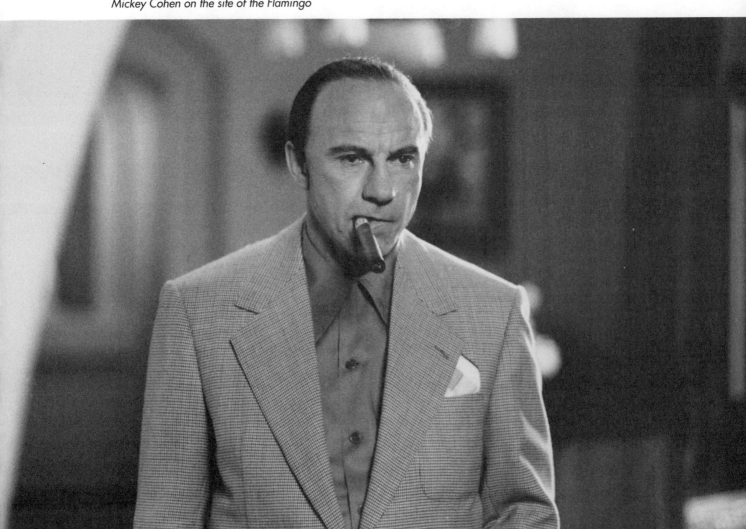

BUGSY

Mickey, what do you really think about this guy David, the architect?

MICKEY

What about him?

BUGSY

You think he's any good? There's something I don't like about him. I mean…what is it with this fuckin' red necktie?

MICKEY

Hey. He's an architect. What do you want?

BUGSY

I want you to keep your eye on him. There's something about him that makes me nervous. What's his history? How did we get him?

MICKEY

Ben, don't do this. You'll drive yourself nuts.

BUGSY

I have to know the truth, Mickey.

MICKEY

The truth is: who the fuck ever knows anything about what's going on with any broad?

BUGSY

I have to know the truth about *her*.

Bugsy looks at Virginia and then at George, who is staring at her as she speaks to David and writes a check which she hands to Del.

BUGSY
(to George)
What's the matter, George? What are you looking at?

GEORGE

Nothing.

BUGSY

Why do you say "nothing"? You were looking at Virginia.

GEORGE

She was talking. It's natural to look at someone who is talking.

BUGSY

You were thinking something.

GEORGE

Okay. I was thinking — do you really trust a dame with that kind of money? I've never known a broad I'd give more than a couple of hundred bucks to for a dress and a negligee.

BUGSY

I'm not giving it to a "dame." I'm not giving it to a "broad." I'm giving it to Virginia and I trust her completely.

Moe emerges, addresses Bugsy.

MOE

Meyer would like to talk to you.

As Bugsy goes to the den, Mickey notices a taxi pulling up outside and moves to investigate.

INT. BUGSY'S HOUSE - DEN - DAY

Bugsy picks up the phone. Moe is standing nearby.

BUGSY
(into the phone)
Meyer!…Where are you? Miami? …Havana! What a fabulous connection!…Of course I plan to be at Charlie's farewell deportation party. I'm just glad he's out of jail…No one feels sicker about Harry Greenberg than I do. I brought him in with us…I know that, Meyer, and when you find him you'll just have to do what you have to do…*Overages?…What* overages?

EXT. BUGSY'S HOUSE - DAY

Harry Greenberg is paying the TAXI DRIVER.

TAXI DRIVER

You do know who this house belongs to, don't you? Bugsy Siegel.

Bugsy at home on the phone with Meyer

HARRY

Shhh. Don't ever call him that.

TAXI DRIVER

Aaah. Everyone calls him that out here.

HARRY

Not to his face. I'll bet my life on that. Things may have changed, but they haven't changed *that* much.

INT. BUGSY'S HOUSE - DEN - DAY

Bugsy continues on the phone with Meyer. The temperature has been raised.

BUGSY

You're missing the point, Meyer. I'd be happy to come back to a deportation party for Charlie to pay my respects and say good-bye —but not to haggle about some petty overages on the Flamingo. Did they ask Michelangelo how much the Sistine Chapel would cost to paint? Did they ask Shakespeare how much it would cost to write *Macbeth*?…If it costs a little more, then it costs a little more. Yes…Yes…I'll see you in New York.

Bugsy hangs up the phone.

BUGSY

I'm dealing with a bunch of bloodless bureaucrats!

MICKEY

Ben, Harry Greenberg is here.

BUGSY

Where?

MICKEY

In the hallway.

INT. BUGSY'S HOUSE - HALLWAY - DAY

Bugsy approaches Harry.

BUGSY

Hi, Harry.

HARRY

Ben! What a sight for sore eyes you are! I hope you ain't angry with me for intruding.

(Bugsy just looks at Harry)

I had nowhere else to go.

BUGSY

You did the right thing, Harry. Are you tired?

HARRY

Beat.

BUGSY

I've got an extra bedroom upstairs. Why don't you take a nap and we'll talk when you wake up.

HARRY

Thanks, Ben. I need a rest.

BUGSY

(points the way)

It's the one on the left.

Harry follows the directions. Virginia comes up to Ben.

VIRGINIA

What are you going to do?

BUGSY

(with Harry on his mind)

About what?

VIRGINIA

The money.

BUGSY

I have it.

VIRGINIA

How can you have it? You don't even know how much you need.

BUGSY

You want to pull out?

VIRGINIA

No. It's just that you seemed so sure of everything...and now —

BUGSY

I *am* sure. Of the *end*. Just a little mystery about how to get there. But that's the *fun*. Right?

He looks into her eyes.

EXT. BUGSY'S HOUSE - NIGHT

The house is quiet. The lights are on downstairs and off upstairs except for one dim light.

INT. BUGSY'S HOUSE - HARRY'S BEDROOM - NIGHT

Harry is asleep. The door opens and Bugsy comes in. Bugsy stands over Harry, watching. Finally, Harry wakes up. He is dressed.

HARRY

(looking at Bugsy, confused)

Ben. I thought I was dreaming.

BUGSY

That's okay. I always think I'm dreaming. I couldn't get through one day if I didn't.

HARRY

Yeah. That's true, Ben. So what do you think? Am I dreaming or am I really out in Hollywood with you?

BUGSY

You're here, Harry.

HARRY

Thank God! If I was anywhere else, I'd be dead. I screwed up, Ben. I'm so stupid. I never wanted to hurt nobody, except the people you told me to hurt, 'cause they was no fuckin' good.

BUGSY

You talked?

HARRY

I talked, Ben. But not about you. I told the guy you were a prince.

BUGSY

What guy?

HARRY

The assistant I told you about. Allen Stein. The Jewish kid from Bedford Avenue. Nice fella. You know the family.

BUGSY

You talked about Charlie?

HARRY

Yeah. But Charlie don't love you, Ben. He pretends he loves you. But he really don't. None of them loves you. You know why? 'Cause you ain't like them. They all think you're crazy. They don't understand you the way I do.

BUGSY

What do you want me to do for you, Harry?

HARRY

I thought maybe somehow I could work out here for you, incognito like.

BUGSY

It's tough to be incognito in Hollywood.

HARRY

I know. Just an idea. Another bad idea. What should I do?

BUGSY

(a deep sigh)

Take a drive with me.

HARRY

Oh, boy! I love drivin' at night. Especially when someone else is drivin'. I've loved that since I was a kid.

BUGSY

I wish you hadn't done what you did, Harry.

Bugsy is almost in tears.

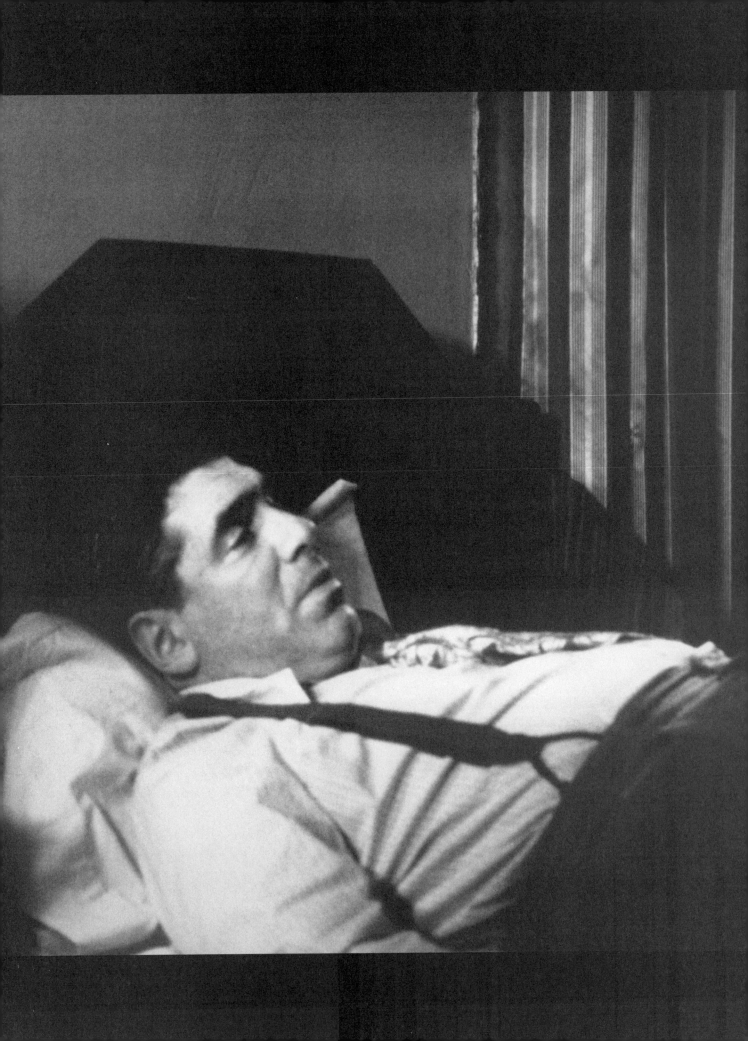

Colleague Harry Greenberg (Elliott Gould) is questioned by a saddened Bugsy

INT. BUGSY'S HOUSE - LIVING ROOM - NIGHT

Virginia is reading some design plans for the Flamingo as Bugsy and Harry come in from upstairs.

> **BUGSY**
> (to Virginia)
> This is Harry Greenberg, one of my oldest friends in the world.
> (to Harry)
> Virginia Hill.

> **HARRY**
> Joey A.'s girl! Sure. We met at the Copa years ago.

Bugsy forces himself to ignore Harry's remark to Virginia.

> **BUGSY**
> Harry and I are gonna take a little drive.

> **VIRGINIA**
> I'll come with you.

> **BUGSY**
> It's better if you stay here. I won't be long.

> **VIRGINIA**
> I'd rather come along with you.

> **BUGSY**
> I'd rather you stay here.

> **VIRGINIA**
> I thought you wanted to be with me all the time.

> **BUGSY**
> Will you please let us take a fucking drive alone?

> **VIRGINIA**
> You can take your whole life alone, if that's what you want.

> **BUGSY**
> You want to come along? Come along.

VIRGINIA

I'll be right there. I've gotta get my coat and purse.

EXT. BUGSY'S CAR - WAREHOUSE AREA - NIGHT

Bugsy drives with Virginia seated in between him and Harry.

HARRY

(to Virginia)

So you seen much of Joey recently?

VIRGINIA

Not for quite a while.

HARRY

Me, neither. But I haven't seen any of the guys since I messed up. Joey was always a real sharp dresser. Nice wavy head of hair, too.

BUGSY

(to Harry)

Harry, Virginia is going to be my wife.

HARRY

Yeah? No kidding. Congratulations!…What happened to Esta?

BUGSY

Nothing happened to Esta.

HARRY

Oh *good*, that's a relief. I thought she died.

(he thinks)

So what happened to her?

BUGSY

We're getting a divorce.

VIRGINIA

They're getting a divorce—only Esta doesn't know it yet.

BUGSY

Why do you always have to take these little digs at me? Esta's my friend. Accept that. She's a good person, she's the mother of my two daughters, and she isn't any threat to you. And I'm going to divorce her.

VIRGINIA

I'm sorry. I was out of line.

Bugsy looks at Virginia as though he doesn't believe his ears. He drives on, looks at Harry, who is smiling beatifically.

HARRY

You two seem like a very happy couple. It's nice to see that.

Bugsy pulls up at the foot of a road, leading to a warehouse.

BUGSY

(to Virginia)
Wait here. And please don't argue with me about it.

EXT. TRAIN TRESTLE ROAD AND BUGSY'S CAR - NIGHT

Bugsy looks at Harry. They walk up a quiet path. Virginia, who has no idea what is about to happen, sits impatiently in the car.

Virginia gets out of the car, paces back and forth; she walks along and yells.

VIRGINIA

(calling out)
Ben. What the hell's going on out there? Ben! Ben!

Two pops are heard echoing, three seconds apart.

VIRGINIA

(nearing panic)
Ben? Ben! BEN!!

Virginia starts running toward the spot where Bugsy and Harry disappeared. Bugsy is coming back quickly toward the car, and they almost collide.

BUGSY

What are you doing? I told you to wait in the car. Get back. Quick!

VIRGINIA

Where's Harry?

BUGSY

Get in the car.

She looks at him. They both get into Bugsy's car and drive off.

INT. BUGSY'S CAR - DRIVING - NIGHT

Bugsy drives Virginia in silence. Virginia, distraught, tries to compose herself. As if to himself, Bugsy starts to speak — almost inaudibly.

BUGSY

Twenty dwarves took turns doing handstands on the carpet...
Twenty dwarves took turns doing handstands on the carpet...

EXT./INT. OCEAN LINER - DAY

A huge, catered, opulently organized farewell deportation party for Charlie with musicians and dancing. All members of the gang whom we've met previously are in attendance as well as what looks to be the entire line from the Latin Quarter. Bugsy is confronting Charlie, who is holding court, surrounded by Meyer, Vito, Frank, Moe, Joey A., and Gus Greenbaum.

CHARLIE

This fuckin' building was supposed to cost us one million dollars and all of a sudden it's climbing through the fuckin' roof!

BUGSY

We're spending what we need to spend to do it right.

CHARLIE

Who's "we"? You want to spend more than a million dollars, *you* spend it.

BUGSY

What are you getting at, Charlie? Do you want out?

CHARLIE

Of course, I want out. You think *anybody* wanted a piece of this screwball building of yours? You think *Vito* wanted it? Or Frank? Or Joey A.? Or Meyer? A hotel in the middle of the Mojave desert five hundred miles away from the nearest toilet bowl? I approved the million dollars because you did a great job setting things up in Los Angeles. But a gift of a million dollars is one thing—

BUGSY

What do you you mean, "gift"? It was no—

Meyer (standing, right), Joey A., and associates during the shipboard farewell deportation party for Charles "Lucky" Luciano (Bill Graham)

Meyer addresses Charlie and Bugsy and sets the stage...

...for Charlie, who castigates Bugsy for overages on the building of the Flamingo

CHARLIE

Let me finish. A gift of a million dollars is one thing, a blank check made out to someone who hasn't said no to himself on anything in twenty-five years is pushing it too far. And this movie star Hollywood shit that's got into you is no good. We're private. We don't want anybody lookin' at us and takin' our picture and writin' stories. It's bad enough the way it is. This Flamingo thing could take it out of control.

BUGSY

You finished? First of all, the Flamingo will be a legitimate operation. There won't *be* anything to hide. Secondly, the money you and Meyer put up was no gift. It was a *favor* that *I* let *you* come in on.

CHARLIE

Fine. Then let us out. Now. At cost. No profits.

BUGSY

You want out? YOU'RE OUT!

MEYER

Fellas, fellas, fellas! Stop all this nonsense. This is a farewell party for old friends. Old, dear friends.

CHARLIE

Fuck old friends. You don't tell old friends a deal's gonna cost a million dollars and then come back and say it's two or three or four or any other shit like that. Not to Charlie Luciano you don't.

BUGSY

We're speaking different languages, Charlie. That's the problem. We're speaking different languages.

MEYER

Benny. Please. Answer a question for me. What is the most that this hotel could possibly cost?

BUGSY

Three million. Tops!

CHARLIE

Three million?

MEYER

You sure? Because from the stories I'm hearing—with all the imported palm trees and Italian marble and whatnot—people are saying the place could go to four, maybe five million.

BUGSY

Three million is the maximum the Flamingo would possibly cost.

CHARLIE

I don't give a fuck. I only approved one—*one*—not *three*!

MEYER

Ben, how much money do you have?

BUGSY

In cash?

MEYER

That's what we use, isn't it?

BUGSY

It fluctuates.

MEYER

Well, given all the fluctuations and permutations and titillations that you can imagine, how much actual real cash can you get your hands on today?

BUGSY

Three. Three-fifty. Maybe four. Maybe four hundred thousand.

MEYER

You can't pin it down a little better? We're not talking about nickels here.

BUGSY

Let's say three. No—four! Let's say four!

MEYER

(ponders; to Bugsy)

Lookit. I got an idea. You put up four hundred thousand and the two of us will put up four apiece. Plus I'll put up the other eight hundred thousand in escrow in case the hotel balloons to three.

CHARLIE

What the fuck am I doing puttin' in an extra four hundred thousand when I don't want in what I already have in?

MEYER

You think *I* want to throw in this extra *million two* that I'm throwin' in? Whatever we want or don't want, it doesn't matter now. We're stuck. So we do what we have to do to make it work.
(to Bugsy)
Within reason.

CHARLIE

You call any of this reason? I find the whole thing disgusting...
(to Bugsy)
And if it *is* more than three million, *God* won't be able to bail you out of this.

BUGSY

No problem.

CHARLIE

There's one other thing, Ben.
(Bugsy turns back)
The broad.

BUGSY

What broad?

CHARLIE

Why would you want some broad handling our money?

BUGSY

She's not a broad. People are going to have to speak with respect about Virginia. She's going to be my wife.

Charlie looks to Meyer, who shrugs.

CHARLIE

Congratulations. I'm sure she'll make a terrific Mrs. Siegel. I hope you know what you're doing.

As Bugsy prepares to leave the ship, he sees Joey A., who is making an aggressive move on CHERYL, a showgirl. Bugsy approaches Joey.

Bugsy parries Joey's rage over his romance with Virginia

BUGSY

Joey, can I speak to you alone?

JOEY A.

What do you want? I'm busy.

BUGSY

It'll only take a second.

JOEY A.

Make it quick.

(to Cheryl)

Don't you dare move now, Cheryl. I'll get rid of this guy before you have time to blink your pretty eyes.

Bugsy guides Joey A. into a nearby area of the party.

BUGSY

Considering the insulting word you used to describe Virginia, I think you owe both of us an apology.

JOEY A.

You do? Well, why don't you try sucking your apology outta my dick?

BUGSY

Joey! What a thing to say…Okay.

JOEY A.

What?

BUGSY

Here. You want to see it? Go ahead. Take a look.

Bugsy starts to unzip. When Joey looks down, Bugsy knees him in the face and then — in swift and mercilessly brutal fashion — rattles, batters, and stomps Joey A. into pulpy unconsciousness. Bugsy seems possessed, as if carrying out a mission. He adjusts his hair in a mirror, then looks down.

BUGSY

Can you hear me? You're very lucky I haven't had a lot to drink today. Your apology is accepted.

EXT. BROADWAY RESTAURANT - NIGHT

Jubilation. Wild celebrating of V-J Day.

INT. BROADWAY RESTAURANT - NIGHT

Bugsy eats dinner with Esta, Millicent and Barbara at a corner table.

> **B U G S Y**
>
> What I was thinking is…was…that…if…
> (to Millicent)
> Chew it well. Don't swallow it until you've chewed it. What I was thinking…
> (to waiter)
> Could you bring some more water over and…
> (to the girls and Esta)
> Anyone want anything else?

> **M I L L I C E N T**
>
> You just asked us that a minute ago, Daddy.

> **B U G S Y**
>
> Right. What was I saying?

> **E S T A**
>
> Whatever it is you've been trying to say all night. Our plans for moving.

> **B U G S Y**
>
> Right. Umm…see, I'm trying to work out what would be best for…I mean, I'm gonna be spending all my time in Las Vegas, which is nothing but a sand dune right now, so I'll just be there alone, with the workmen. Of course, you could stay at my house in Los Angeles if you wanted to, but it really wouldn't make sense because I won't be there at all myself. So maybe the best idea would be to stay here, where you feel at home.

> **E S T A**
>
> And see you for a day or two every couple of years?

Bugsy says nothing. Millicent is hurt and disappointed. Barbara looks sick. They all eat in uneasy silence. Finally, Esta, who can barely contain her tears, gets up shakily.

ESTA

Excuse me.

She rushes off to the ladies' room. Bugsy follows her.

INT. BROADWAY RESTAURANT - LADIES' ROOM VESTIBULE - NIGHT

BUGSY

I'm sorry. I—

ESTA

You've found somebody, haven't you?
> (Bugsy looks at her, then looks down)

If you want to be with her, and not with me, I want a divorce.
> (she waits, trembling)

Is that what *you* want?…Is it?

BUGSY

I want to take care of you and the children. I want—

ESTA

A divorce. You want a divorce, don't you?

Bugsy still doesn't answer her. She slaps him hard across the face.

ESTA

> (in a harsh whisper)

Answer me!

Bugsy still can't answer. Esta slaps him across the face again…even harder.

ESTA

You want a divorce! Say it!

BUGSY

I do.

Esta starts to break down. Bugsy holds her, strokes her head. Finally, she pushes him away.

ESTA

Don't come out for a minute.

Esta goes out, leaving Bugsy alone in the ladies' room.

Bugsy, after Esta walks out on him

INT./EXT. BROADWAY RESTAURANT - DINING AREA - NIGHT

Bugsy approaches the front window of the restaurant and through it sees the wildly celebrating V-J Day crowd just in time to see Esta putting Barbara and Millicent into a taxi. Bugsy watches the taxi disappear into the mob.

EXT. DESERT - ESTABLISHING SHOT OF CONSTRUCTION SITE - DAY

EXT. FLAMINGO HOTEL SITE - LAS VEGAS DESERT - DAY

Bugsy, Virginia (carrying notebooks filled with figures), Del Webb, Chick, and David examine the site as the construction workers continue working. We see wood, glass, marble, concrete, rubber, paint and other materials. The structure of the hotel is already clear, twenty-five percent toward completion. Bugsy paces animatedly, looking into everything (and everybody's job).

> **BUGSY**
> (to all of them)
> Isn't this the most spectacular sight you've ever seen? It's breathtaking. It's vast and intimate, it's original...it's...
> (suddenly, Bugsy is seized by a thought)
> Where's the pool?

DAVID

Right through here.

BUGSY

But how do I see the pool from the casino?

DAVID

The pool from the casino?

DEL
(to Bugsy)

Ben, your point was to get sun down on the pool unobstructed.
That's why you told us to move it. Remember?

BUGSY
(ignoring them)

I thought we were going to be able to see the pool from the casino.

DAVID

I'm afraid that's impossible.

BUGSY
(oblivious)

So that wherever you're standing in the casino, there's the pool
right in front of you.

DEL

I think the problem we have here is —
(to David)
Correct me if I'm wrong, David.
(to Bugsy)
— this is a bearing wall.

BUGSY

Okay. Just get rid of it.

DAVID

But it's supporting the structure.

VIRGINIA

You see, Ben, what David's saying? The wall —

In Las Vegas, Bugsy supervises the construction of the Flamingo…

…as Mickey arrives to give him news about Virginia…

BUGSY

I got the point, Virginia. I don't need a fucking translator. I also don't need you to parrot everything this guy says.
(to David)
Just get rid of that wall.

DEL

Well, what we could do is make the wall glass. Then we could see the pool from the casino. But it would be expensive. We would have to install a header beam.

BUGSY

There you go! A header beam! You saved the day, Del.

DEL

I must tell you, Ben, that with all these overages we're picking up, we're looking at a budget now that's right up near—
(he turns to Virginia)
Four and a half million.

B U G S Y

No problem.

At this point two official-looking cars pull up and four FEDERAL MARSHALS get out.

D E L

Who the hell are they?

B U G S Y

Federal marshals.

F E D E R A L   M A R S H A L   # 1

Bugsy Siegel, I have a warrant for your arrest.

B U G S Y

I don't know anyone named that. Here or anywhere else.

Marshal #2 whispers into the ear of Marshal #1.

...while workmen struggle to meet their deadline

FEDERAL MARSHAL #1

Benjamin Siegel. I have a warrant for your arrest and a court order to transport you across state lines to the proper authorities in the County of Los Angeles in the State of California.

BUGSY

What's the charge?

FEDERAL MARSHAL #1

Homicide.

BUGSY

Of?

FEDERAL MARSHAL #1

Harry Greenberg.

BUGSY

My friend Harry Greenberg?

FEDERAL MARSHAL #1

If he was your friend, I'd sure hate to be your enemy.

FEDERAL MARSHAL #2

I'm sorry, sir, I'm gonna have to cuff you.

VIRGINIA

Ben, I'm going with you.

FEDERAL MARSHAL #1

No, you're not.

Bugsy is handcuffed and loaded into the car.

EXT. LOS ANGELES COURTHOUSE - DAY

Bugsy, handcuffed, is led inside for his arraignment. Between his exiting of the police car and his entrance into the courthouse, Bugsy is bombarded by flashbulbs popping and crowds of reporters yelling questions: "Did you kill him?" "Are you guilty?" "Is it true that Harry Greenberg was going to testify against all your friends?" Several reporters yell "Bugsy!" Bugsy stops at the doorway of the courthouse and police escorting him stop too. Bugsy faces the throng.

BUGSY

I only have two things to say. First, the name is *Ben*. Benjamin. From the Bible. Secondly, I'll see you all at the opening of the Flamingo on Christmas day.

He smiles and goes inside.

INT. LOS ANGELES COURTHOUSE - DAY

As Bugsy is moved down the corridor, Hartman approaches the cops escorting Bugsy.

HARTMAN

I'm Assistant District Attorney Hartman. I'm in charge of this case. You can leave the prisoner with me.
> (to Bugsy)

Come this way.

Bugsy walks with Hartman, who stops at an empty courtroom and addresses the SECURITY GUARD.

HARTMAN

Don't let anybody else inside.

SECURITY GUARD

Yes, sir.

Hartman holds the door open for Bugsy, who goes inside.

INT. LOS ANGELES COURTHOUSE - COURTROOM - DAY

Bugsy finds McWilde in the courtroom.

BUGSY

What the hell is going on? Thirty thousand dollars cash to your "campaign" isn't enough to keep me on the streets?

McWILDE

Shh! The walls are thin in here. I *had* to have you arrested, Ben.

BUGSY

What do you mean you *had* to?

Following the arrest for Harry Greenberg's murder, Bugsy arrives at the Los Angeles Courthouse

McWILDE

Hearst. He's splashing it all over the front pages. I couldn't just ignore it.

BUGSY

Why not? Where's the witness? There's no case without a witness.

McWILDE

(hesitates a bit; looks around; whispers)

The taxi driver.

BUGSY

What taxi driver?

McWILDE

The driver who dropped Harry Greenberg off at your house the day that he was killed.

BUGSY

You have his name?

McWilde nods almost imperceptibly.

BUGSY

I would like that information accidentally to find it's way into the hands of Mickey Cohen.

McWILDE

It can be arranged. But I *warn* you. Nothing nasty. I won't be—

BUGSY

You don't have to "warn" me about anything. Just give the name to Mickey Cohen.

INT. LOS ANGELES COURTHOUSE - COURTROOM - DAY

Bugsy, in a different courtroom, stands as the JUDGE addresses him.

JUDGE

Mr. Siegel, considering the utmost gravity of the charges entered against you—murder in the first degree—I hereby order you held without bail.

The Judge slams the gavel.

INT. LOS ANGELES COUNTY JAIL - CORRIDOR - DAY

An elegantly appointed, and lavishly supplied, supper table — of the sort used in fine hotels for room service — is being wheeled down the jailhouse corridor and then into Bugsy's cell by Tony, the waiter from Ciro's.

INT. LOS ANGELES COUNTY JAIL - BUGSY'S CELL - DAY

Bugsy, dressed in a silk robe and wearing an ascot, sits in an inordinately well-appointed jail cell, scrutinizing a front-page photograph of himself in the *Examiner* whose accompanying headline reads: "BUGSY SIEGEL ARRESTED FOR MURDER — McWilde Hauls In Gangster From Las Vegas." Tony removes the hot dishes from the heated compartment.

> **T O N Y**
>
> Rare steak…plain spinach…

> **B U G S Y**
>
> Tony, I want to ask you something. Be honest with me. Do you
> think this picture makes me look pale?

The phone rings and Bugsy picks it up before Tony has a chance to answer. As Bugsy speaks, Tony continues to uncover dishes.

> **B U G S Y**
>
> Hello?…Mickey! Where are you? Las Vegas?…If you're still here
> how can you be watching Virginia? Who's watching her? I want
> you to do it personally. How do you know he's not going to try
> something funny with her?…Have you done anything about the
> cab driver problem?…Good. By the way, did you see the picture
> in the *Examiner* today? It's the worst one yet — I got no tan. I look
> like a fucking marshmallow!…Do you mean that or are you just
> trying to make me feel good?…

Tony walks over to Bugsy for an approval of the wine.

> **B U G S Y**
> (shoving the newspaper in front Tony again; to Tony)
> What do *you* think? Pale or not pale?

> **T O N Y**
>
> Not pale.

BUGSY
(to Mickey)

Stay on top of Virginia. I want constant reports. I feel very isolated in here.

EXT. LAS VEGAS - FLAMINGO CONSTRUCTION SITE - DAY

Virginia arrives at the Flamingo in Chick's red Cadillac, driven by Chick. A vicious sandstorm makes visibility and movement difficult, but the crew is struggling to work under Del's supervision. Virginia and Chick get out of the car. Virginia sees Meyer, who, fighting the wind, is examining the demolished wall of the casino, as if surveying the ruins of a bombed village. As she approaches him, he seems both lost in thought and bothered by the elements. Mickey paces in the background.

VIRGINIA

I think you'll be surprised at how things will shape up before we're through.

MEYER

He's talking about opening at Christmas?

VIRGINIA

Oh, he's *going* to open at Christmas. Ben is absolutely determined about that.

MEYER

"Absolutely determined…Absolutely determined…"

VIRGINIA
(firmly)

It'll open on time.

She stares into Meyer's eyes. Meyer looks back at her, smiles faintly—

MEYER

You've changed a lot since I first met you.

Meyer wanders off. He ponders the demolished wall.

MEYER

What happened here?

VIRGINIA

Ben wanted to be able to see the pool from the casino and the way it had come out, you couldn't.

Meyer looks at Virginia as if to say: "So he tore the whole building apart?" Meyer ducks under the beam.

MEYER

This is unusual.

Meyer wanders off in the sandstorm. Virginia watches him as he goes over and starts talking with urgency to Mickey.

INT. LOS ANGELES COUNTY JAIL - BUGSY'S CELL - DAY

Bugsy and Virginia are seated at the dinner table. Tony readies their dinner on the supper cart.

BUGSY
(to Virginia)
You called to tell me you were leaving Las Vegas but you didn't tell me that Meyer was there?

Bugsy, almost unconsciously, hands Tony a hundred-dollar tip.

GUARD

Thank you, Mr. Siegel.

Bugsy, focused on Virginia, pursues.

BUGSY

I'm asking you a question.

VIRGINIA

I thought it would be better if I told you in person.

BUGSY

But why didn't you tell me then?

VIRGINIA

What's the difference, Ben? I'm here. I'm telling you now.

BUGSY

He saw the Flamingo? What did he say?

VIRGINIA

He said he was worried about the cost.

BUGSY

What else did he say?

VIRGINIA

I didn't discuss anything else with him. He talked to Del Webb.

BUGSY

Did he ask any specific questions?

VIRGINIA

No. But he seemed curious about the demolished wall.

BUGSY

Did he ask about the header beam?

VIRGINIA

Not exactly. But he ducked under it.

BUGSY

Ducked?

VIRGINIA

It's low.

BUGSY

How low?

VIRGINIA

Too low. Unless you happen to be a five-foot, one-inch gambler.
But they're going to fix it.

BUGSY

What was Meyer's general attitude?

VIRGINIA

Concern. But he never raised his voice. He was very nice. The way
he's always been.

BUGSY

Always? What do you mean "always?"

VIRGINIA

Always. It means "as in the past."

BUGSY

You didn't know him in the past.

VIRGINIA

Sure I did. Through Joey.

BUGSY

Did you fuck him?

VIRGINIA

You know I did. Why do you ask me that now?

BUGSY

You fucked Meyer?

VIRGINIA

Oh, stop it. Don't be disgusting. I meant Joey and you know it.

BUGSY

Why is fucking Meyer any more disgusting than fucking Joey? Is the thought of fucking Joey not disgusting?

VIRGINIA

Ben, you have to stop this bullshit.

BUGSY

(in a crescendo of fury)

Listen. If they can't get it right, then let them tear down the whole fucking thing and start from scratch! You hear me? I did not come this far to end up with a casino that doesn't let you see the pool. If you have to tear down the whole casino, tear down the whole casino!

VIRGINIA

Ben—

BUGSY

TEAR IT DOWN!

VIRGINIA

Ben. The cost is going haywire.

BUGSY

What is this? Are you on their side?

VIRGINIA

Don't ever say that to me again.

BUGSY

Fuck Meyer Lansky! The hell with Las Vegas! The hell with the Flamingo.

Bugsy gets up and lurches over to the bars. Virginia suddenly takes a calm, quiet, affectionate tone as she walks over to the bars next to Bugsy.

VIRGINIA

I spent three minutes with Meyer in the middle of a sand blizzard trying to say the things I thought *you* would say to keep things from seeming any worse than they already did. He even said I *sounded* like you.

BUGSY

I just wish the two of us could be alone on Coney Island eating a couple of fucking hot dogs at Nathan's.

Virginia nods tenderly. Bugsy leans toward her, presses her to him.

INT. UNION STATION - DAY

Mickey and the taxi driver, carrying two suitcases, enter the train station.

They walk up through the tunnel as they head toward the train platform.

MICKEY

You're going to like Kansas City. There's a lot of fun in that city.

Mickey stuffs an envelope full of cash into the taxi driver's hand and pushes him onto the train.

EXT. LOS ANGELES COUNTY JAIL - DAY

Bugsy and George (carrying four of Bugsy's suitcases) are walking down the steps.

GEORGE

Cary Grant, Gary Cooper, and Clark Gable. They're all gonna be there!

BUGSY

This is going to be the biggest, star-studded opening gala in history! You're a prince, Georgie boy.

GEORGE

Anything for my pal.

A limousine is parked in front. The rear door opens, revealing Meyer.

BUGSY

I'll see you back at the house, George. Thanks.

GEORGE

You're welcome. If you have any more luggage, feel free to carry it yourself.

George goes off to his car as Bugsy gets into Meyer's limousine.

INT. MEYER'S LIMOUSINE - DRIVING - DAY

Bugsy climbs in next to Meyer, who speaks to the CHAUFFEUR.

MEYER

Take me to Union Station and then take Mr. Siegel wherever he wants to go.

CHAUFFEUR

Yes, sir, Mr. Lansky.

Meyer and Bugsy look straight ahead silently for a few moments. Finally, Meyer speaks.

MEYER

The Flamingo's gonna come in at six million, Ben.

BUGSY

Meyer, listen, anyone who —

MEYER

Ben. I'm on your side. I'm doing what I can. Stop trying to fool me. And stop trying to fool yourself.

There is a long pause. Finally, Meyer speaks.

MEYER

Lookit. You need three million dollars. If you can come up with two million, I'll come up with one. Charlie knows nothing about this. It's between you and me. Can you come up with that kind of money?

BUGSY

No problem.

MEYER

Will you stop that, please? Will you stop with the "no problems"? Think for a second. What are you going to do to get the money? All your property—the house in Scarsdale, the cars, stocks, bonds—it all belongs to Esta and the girls now—isn't that correct?

BUGSY

Absolutely.

MEYER

Then how are you going to get two million dollars?

BUGSY

I'll sell things.

MEYER

What things?

BUGSY

I'll sell my house. I'll sell everything *in* my house.

MEYER

Sounds to me like about two hundred thousand—tops. Where's the other million eight comin' from?

Bugsy doesn't answer.

MEYER

You always protected me, Ben. You were always behind me…But I can't protect you.

BUGSY

My shares.

MEYER

What about them?

BUGSY

I own a third of the hotel. I'll sell it.

MEYER

That's all you've got, Ben. You'll end up with nothing. After all this…Nothing.

BUGSY

But the Flamingo will be there. That's not nothing.

They drive in silence. The limousine pulls up in front of Union Station. Meyer hands Bugsy a briefcase.

MEYER

Add your two to this.

As Meyer gets out of the limousine, without looking at Bugsy, he says (almost to himself):

MEYER

I miss you, Benny.

Meyer closes the door and walks into Union Station.

INT./EXT. LOS ANGELES/LAS VEGAS MONTAGE

A MONTAGE of auctioning, building and selling — connected by the SIGHT and SOUND of a gavel banging (followed by the cry of "sold!") and the SIGHT and SOUND of hammers striking nails into wood in construction work on the rapidly progressing Flamingo. The auction involves the sale of all of Bugsy's possessions and, finally, the sale of the house itself. Interspersed as well are several cuts of Bugsy selling shares in the Flamingo (in the form of highly decorative but official-looking stock certificates reading "Flamingo Hotel Corporation") to a wide variety of people, including McWilde, Dorothy, and Tony — culminating in a cut of Bugsy handing a check and a stock certificate to a somewhat relieved (by the check) Del Webb.

INT. BILTMORE HEALTH CLUB - DAY

Mickey, Bugsy, and George are lying on lounge chairs at the Biltmore Health Club under sunlamps with cucumbers on their eyes and facial creams and oils generously applied (olive oil is in their hair, which is slicked back under stockings). They wear terry-cloth robes.

BUGSY

I've decided to sell both of you ten percent of the Flamingo.

GEORGE

How much?

BUGSY

Sixty thousand each.

MICKEY

But I thought all the shares in the Flamingo had already been sold!

BUGSY

If I'm still *selling* them, then they can't all have been sold.

EXT. AIRPLANE IN THE SKY - DAY

Bugsy's POV from the plane to the Flamingo under construction. Bugsy is elated at the sight.

EXT. FLAMINGO LANDING STRIP - DAY

The plane lands at an extremely modest airstrip/airport. Bugsy and STEVE, the pilot, head toward the small structure, which, although no larger than a garage, serves as the terminal.

BUGSY

We've gotta have a whole fleet of planes for Christmas, Steve. I'm flying up half of Los Angeles.

STEVE

Just give me a couple of weeks' notice and the cash in advance and you've got the whole air force if you want, Mr. Siegel.

Chick and Virginia pull up in Chick's red Cadillac convertible. Virginia climbs out and meets Bugsy halfway.

BUGSY

What'll it take?

VIRGINIA

For what?

BUGSY

To get you up there. You've got to see it from the air. It's a palace in the middle of nowhere.

VIRGINIA

No. No.

BUGSY

Come on.

VIRGINIA

Ben.

Virginia gestures to the car and starts toward it. Bugsy turns to Steve.

BUGSY

Forget it, Steve.

Bugsy follows Virginia to the car.

EXT. LAS VEGAS - FLAMINGO HOTEL - DAY

Bugsy and Virginia are in the midst of frenzied last-minute preparations. Mickey's car pulls up.

BUGSY
(to Virginia)

Hey! Look who's here.

Mickey joins Bugsy while Virginia stops to talk to Del.

MICKEY

Hello, Ben.

BUGSY

Miss the desert?

MICKEY
(somber)

That isn't why I came.

BUGSY

Why did you?

Mickey gives a hint of a nod toward Virginia. Bugsy is alert with suspicion.

BUGSY

What did she do?

MICKEY

She fucked you.

BUGSY

What are you talking about? How?

MICKEY

There's a numbered bank account in Switzerland with almost two million dollars in it.

BUGSY

So?

MICKEY

It's hers.

BUGSY

I'm sure there are a *lot* of two-million-dollar numbered bank accounts in Switzerland.

MICKEY

Yeah. But only one that was set up by Joe Epstein of Chicago for Virginia Hill of Beverly Hills.
(Bugsy can't speak)
I seen copies of the deposit records, Ben.

BUGSY

It's a lie, Mickey. And if you repeat it, I'll break your fucking jaw.

Bugsy storms off into the desert, where he paces and kicks the dirt.

Mickey walks into the casino and asks for a drink.

He watches Bugsy off in the desert.

INT. FLAMINGO HOTEL - MONTAGE - DAY

Montage of various background workers painting and making various other preparations for the hotel's opening.

INT. FLAMINGO - LOBBY - NIGHT

Bugsy walks through the lobby amid busy construction and decoration. NATALIE, a self-consciously attractive woman of twenty-one, approaches Bugsy, as Bugsy berates AL, the bartender.

BUGSY

Al, didn't I tell you I didn't want them to show? Move the cases. Move them! Move the goddamn cases.

NATALIE

Mr. Siegel? My name is Natalie St. Clair. Mr. Webb suggested that
I speak to you about the possibility of working at the Flamingo.

BUGSY

As what?

NATALIE

Anything you need.

BUGSY

If you could *invent* a job for yourself, what would it be?

NATALIE

Ummmmmm…Hatcheck girl!

BUGSY

Um…I don't know about that.

NATALIE

Or bartender.

BUGSY

Al, move the goddamn cases.   .
> (to Natalie)

You came from Hollywood?

NATALIE

Uh-huh.

BUGSY

Did you fly here?

NATALIE

I'd love to fly, but I couldn't afford it. I hitchhiked.

From off camera Bugsy—and we—hear Virginia.

VIRGINIA

Looking for a girl who likes to fly?

BUGSY

> (startled; then recovering)

Hi, sugar.

An angry Virginia confronts Bugsy

Virginia continues on without breaking stride. Bugsy follows.

INT. FLAMINGO PENTHOUSE - HALLWAY - NIGHT

Virginia runs down the hallway. Bugsy arrives just in time to see the penthouse door close behind her. He knocks on the door. She doesn't respond.

INT. FLAMINGO - PENTHOUSE - SUITE - LIVING ROOM - NIGHT

Bugsy opens the door with his key and enters.

> **BUGSY**
>
> Come on, Sugar. We don't have time for this.

Virginia throws an ashtray at Bugsy.

> **BUGSY**
>
> Shit, Virginia! You almost hit me in the head again. You almost got me in the same spot you opened up the last time. Couldn't you at least aim at something else? It's depressing. It makes me think we're going around in circles.

> **VIRGINIA**
>
> How do you think it makes *me* feel to watch you running around chasing after some little bimbo!

> **BUGSY**
>
> I wasn't *chasing* her. She's an employee. Del told her —

> **VIRGINIA**
>
> An employee of what?

> **BUGSY**
>
> The Flamingo. She's going to be a hatcheck girl.

Virginia removes her high-heeled shoe and hurls it at Bugsy, barely missing his face, but hitting a crystal vase, knocking it to the ground and shattering it.

> **BUGSY**
>
> What are you doing? That's Baccarat crystal you just shattered.

> **VIRGINIA**
>
> I don't care! You just shattered *us* and that's a little more important.

BUGSY

This is — I just — I'm not going to defend myself anymore. There's nothing to defend myself *about*. A woman wanted a job.

Virginia has begun hastily to pack.

BUGSY

What are you doing?

VIRGINIA

Leaving. And don't try to stop me. I should have gone the day you killed Harry Greenberg. I should have gone the day I met you.

BUGSY

Where do you think you're *going*?

VIRGINIA

Wherever I feel like going.

The answer stops Bugsy cold. His tone and manner change.

BUGSY

Are you going where somebody might know about numbered bank accounts?

Now Virginia is stopped cold.

VIRGINIA

Why don't you just ask what you want to ask?

BUGSY

How much money do you have in your account in Switzerland?

VIRGINIA

Why? Do you want to sell me a few shares in the Flamingo? Bring the percentage sold up to three hundred? Or is it four by now? You gave me five and three-quarters percent. You want to sell me ten? The way you did to your sucker friends?

BUGSY

No. I want you to answer the question I'm really asking. How much money have you stolen from this hotel?

Virginia charges at Bugsy, ramming her finger into Bugsy's chest and face as she speaks with ferocity.

VIRGINIA

Look, I've done a hundred times the amount of work I would've
had to do to justify taking anything I could get my hands on!

BUGSY

How much *did* you get your hands on?

VIRGINIA

Nothing! Not one cent! I *could* have taken a lot! And you never
would have known the difference. Because you're an irresponsible,
unrealistic, unreliable, undependable, philandering fuck! And I'm
crazier than you are to have counted on you for anything. What
the hell was I *doing* here? What was I waiting for? Your *divorce*?
Big deal. As if it's changed a thing! I *should* have taken something!
I should still take something—now, before it's too late, but it isn't
in me. It isn't in me to violate the trust of the one person in my life
I've been stupid enough to give myself to in every way. The one
person I've been stupid enough to love.

BUGSY

How much money do you have in that bank account? How much
did you steal?

VIRGINIA

Damn you!

BUGSY

How much?

Virginia takes her suitcase, picks up her shoe and runs out and slams the door. Bugsy stares at the
shattered splinters of glass. He crosses to the bar and smashes his hand into the wall.

EXT. HAVANA AIRPORT - DAY

A Pan Am flight has landed. Charlie comes down the stairs to a red-carpet greeting. The greeting
party in attendance includes Meyer, Frank, Joey A., Vito, Moe, Albert Anastasia and a host of
other Italian gangsters from different parts of the United States. Meyer and Charlie embrace and
kiss each other on the cheeks.

EXT. HOTEL NACIONAL - HAVANA - DAY

Meyer sits at one end of a long rectangular table and Charlie at the other. On either side, all the
other gangsters are seated. INTERCUT with this scene are shots of Bugsy frantically putting the
final touches on the Flamingo.

CHARLIE

First of all, let me say how much it means to me that all of you have taken the time to fly down here to pay your respects to a lonely Italian exile with a swollen prostate gland.

(laughter in the room)

It breaks my heart that the tragic mess with the Flamingo Hotel is being perpetrated by one of my oldest and dearest friends in the world, Benny Siegel. Here's where we stand right now. The Flamingo is going to open up on Christmas Day, which—from what my hotel friends in the know tell me—is the stupidest fucking time you could ever pick to throw open a new joint to the public. The total cost is now six million dollars, which is five million more than the figure I gave the original okay to. To get the last few million he needed to finish construction, he's had to sell four hundred percent of the hotel. A lot of people who think they've got major shares in this joint are famous individuals like movie stars and wealthy businessmen with political connections who ain't gonna just roll over and get stiffed when their time comes to collect. Not that there's likely to be a time to collect because the chances are the whole thing's gonna be a total fiasco. Now all of this is nothing compared to the most serious matter, which is the question of stealing. My banker friends in Switzerland tell me this Virginia Hill—the broad which Joey used to fuck and which Benny's so head and heels over he's lettin' her change his diapers for him—she's pulled out a couple of million loose change for herself from this here deal. To me, there's a simple basic question that we have to answer: Did this broad steal this money without Benny knowing anything about it or was she just fronting for Benny like a shill?

JOEY A.

Anybody who thinks that Bugsy Siegel isn't the guy that—

MEYER

Benny Siegel. His name is Ben. There's no need for disrespect.

JOEY A.

Yeah? What about his disrespect of *us*! He thought of this, he arranged it, he put the broad up to it and then he pushed the whole thing through. I know the broad and I know him. He did it.

FRANK

Anyways, we can't hit the broad. It's not the gentlemanly thing to do. Benny's gotta take the rap. No matter what.

CHARLIE

I agree with Joey and I agree with Frank. How do all of the rest of you feel?

There is general agreement around the table.

CHARLIE

Meyer?

MEYER

I don't believe that Benny knew a thing about what Virginia Hill was doing. I believe that he was blinded by love. Benny's always put women first—that's what makes him Benny. Only this time it's *one* woman that's got him, instead of the whole damn female race. So I believe Benny would accept anything that broad told him. There's no chance he stole from us and there's no chance he *knew* about any stealing. Going over budget and being—being irresponsible—of course! Who ever said Benny was a numbers man? He's always had one basic problem. He doesn't *respect money*. The truth is he's not even *interested* in money for himself off this deal; he's interested in the *idea*.

Skepticism, even mockery, around the table, especially from Joey.

JOEY A.

What idea?

MEYER

The idea of building something. Making something. Benny's a dreamer.
(there is more cynical contempt)
Lookit, I'm not excusing it, I'm *explaining* it. I'm a businessman. As far as I'm concerned, anything the broad took, Benny's gotta make good on. She's his responsibility.

CHARLIE

What do you want to do about it, Meyer? As a businessman.

MEYER

Give him until Christmas, when the hotel opens. See if it works. If it does, we'll all be happy. Let him pay off her debt.

JOEY A.

What if the Flamingo is a bust?

Meyer (at the head of the table, left) chairs the Havana conference called to determine Bugsy's fate

Everybody waits for Meyer's response.

MEYER

Then I'll handle it myself.

EXT. FLAMINGO - NIGHT

It is Christmas. Torrents of rain are coming down. Bugsy, cigar in his mouth, dressed in white tie and tails, walks — dazed — in the downpour.

INT. FLAMINGO - BUGSY'S PENTHOUSE SUITE - NIGHT

Bugsy, half undressed, drier, ready to change to a new tuxedo, stares at a framed photo of Virginia. Outside it continues to pour, with thunder and lightning.

BUGSY

(to himself)

Twenty dwarves took turns doing handstands on the carpet...Twenty dwarves...Twenty dwarves...

INT. FLAMINGO HOTEL - CASINO - NIGHT

Bugsy enters the casino. Only ten players remain, listlessly pursuing the various games as Bugsy moves from table to table in a near daze. The dealers shuffle idly, the croupier spins the roulette wheel. Mickey and George approach.

MICKEY

Worst luck I've ever seen, Ben.

GEORGE

You can do all kinds of things. But you can't control the weather. No mere mortal ever could. We can't lose heart.

Suddenly there is a bolt of lightning and a blast of thunder and all the lights go out. There is a collective groan emitted from the casino. As it fades down, we hear Bugsy's voice.

BUGSY

I want to thank all of you for having come tonight to make the opening of the Flamingo a success. Due to additional refinements that will make the Flamingo an even greater place to be, I am announcing the temporary closing of the hotel, effective Friday. I will see all of you soon at the grand reopening, the date of which will be announced.

Dominic goes to a pay phone to make a surreptitious call.

DOMINIC

Meyer Lansky is on the phone. He wants to talk to you.

EXT. FLAMINGO AIRSTRIP - DAWN

It is still raining and windy. Bugsy is boarding a small plane. Virginia drives up. Bugsy — stunned — gets out of the plane as Virginia runs up to him.

VIRGINIA

I'm sorry, Ben.

BUGSY

Sorry? For what?

VIRGINIA

I should have been with you.

BUGSY

Well, you're here now. You're the only one.

VIRGINIA

They told me you're going to L.A.

BUGSY

I am. I've got a meeting in a couple hours. Meyer's sending Gus and Moe.

VIRGINIA

Ben, if you're going to L.A. for money, you may not need to.

BUGSY

(a moment)

What do you mean?

Virginia takes the check from her purse and hands it to Bugsy.

BUGSY

Two million dollars? Well...I always said you were a better businessman than I was.

(a beat)

I don't get it.

VIRGINIA
(a moment)
I don't know. I guess I thought it would buy us a couple of hot dogs at Coney Island.

BUGSY
Tell you what. Why don't we just keep it in the bank…We'll save it for a rainy day.

Bugsy tears up the check and throws it away.

BUGSY
I got to go, sugar.

VIRGINIA
Do you want me to come with you?
(she waits)
I'll come with you, okay?

BUGSY
Fly?

VIRGINIA
Yeah.

BUGSY
In this?

VIRGINIA
Yeah.

BUGSY
Get out of here. I'm going to be back in a few hours.

Bugsy looks at Virginia. They hug and kiss, then he turns and climbs onto the plane. Virginia stares at the plane leaving.

VIRGINIA
I love you, Ben.

BUGSY
Will you get out of here.

INT. SEAFOOD GROTTO RESTUARANT - NIGHT

Bugsy, on the phone, sits with Mickey and George.

BUGSY

No. Operator. That's Las Vegas, Nevada. Person to person to Virginia Hill...I know the lines are down.
> (to Mickey and George)

You'd think I was trying to reach a gas station in the Himalayas.
> (back to the operator)

I know there's a windstorm.
> (a beat)

I'd rather hold on.
> (Bugsy turns to George)

What time is is?

GEORGE

Ten twenty-four.

BUGSY

She's not going to have any idea where I am. I told her I'd be back by noon.

GEORGE

It's the weather, Ben. She'll understand. You know, I was thinking about this Washington's Birthday idea for the reopening of the Flamingo and I'm convinced—

BUGSY

What time did you say it was?

GEORGE

Ten twenty-four and ten seconds, and in fifty seconds it'll be ten twenty-five.

BUGSY

> (absorbed; ignoring the sarcasm)

I don't understand this shit with Moe and Gus. First they're meeting me at the L.A. Airport at eight in the morning, then it's three in the afternoon at the Brown Derby, now it's eleven-thirty tonight at Virginia's.

GEORGE

It's the weather, Ben.

BUGSY

Everything's the weather. All of a sudden the weather rules the universe.

GEORGE

Benny! Relax. They're probably waiting for you in front of the door. Now if I could have your undivided attention, I think you'll be interested to know that I spoke to Cary Grant this afternoon and he couldn't have been nicer. He promised to—

BUGSY
(interrupting George; to Mickey)

What do you think?

MICKEY

About what?

BUGSY

Moe and Gus. I've gotta get out of here. I've gotta get back. I'll drive. What do you think?

MICKEY

What is there to think? The wind is blowing. I have no opinion on it.

GEORGE

Benny. You gotta relax. You're gonna have a breakdown.

BUGSY
(into the phone)

Operator...
(a beat)
No operator. I am *going* to hold on.
(a click)

Shit!

EXT. LAS VEGAS DESERT - NIGHT

We see a car moving slowly against a heavy desert sandstorm.

EXT. VIRGINIA'S HOUSE - ESTABLISHING SHOT - NIGHT

Mickey, with Bugsy in the front seat next to him, pulls up in front of Virginia's house. Bugsy, on his own channel, seems oblivious to the arrival at his destination.

BUGSY

You know something, Mickey? You've got Virginia all wrong. She was ready to *fly* for me last night!

MICKEY

I don't want to talk about Virginia, Ben.

BUGSY

All right. Good night.

Bugsy gets out and walks up the front pathway and into the house.

INT. VIRGINIA'S HOUSE - NIGHT

Bugsy enters the house and walks through the foyer and into the living room.

INT. VIRGINIA'S HOUSE - NIGHT

A photograph of Virginia and a model of the Flamingo. Bugsy walks around the living room reading the newspaper and watching his screen test. He walks around the coffee table and stands in front of the sofa. A blast of shots sprays the room. One of them rips Bugsy's eye out. Six others tear through his body. All the shots come from outside. Bugsy slumps back on the sofa, dead.

EXT. FLAMINGO HOTEL - NIGHT

The car pulls up at the entrance. Moe Sedway and Gus Greenbaum enter the Flamingo.

EXT. FLAMINGO LOBBY - NIGHT

Virginia and Del are seated at a table going over figures. Moe and Gus approach.

VIRGINIA

Hi, Moe.

MOE

Virginia, this is Gus Greenbaum. Meyer Lansky sent us. We're taking control of the Flamingo Hotel.

VIRGINIA

Ben Siegel controls the Flamingo.

Virginia, about to hear of Bugsy's death

MOE

Bugsy Siegel is dead. The Flamingo belongs to us.

Virginia is stricken.

VIRGINIA

Excuse me.

Virginia gets up walks out.

EXT. FLAMINGO HOTEL - NIGHT

A violent sandstorm swirls around Virginia, who, dazed, walks out of the entrance of the Flamingo.

VIRGINIA

(looking, calling)

Where's the car? Where's my car? I have to get back to Los Angeles.

The camera pans off the entrance to the highway. The sand and dust continue to blow, and as Virginia's voice starts to fade under the sound of the wind we suddenly see dots of light through the dust and sand and slowly the sound of the wind begins to subside and as the sandstorm clears we read on screen:

One week after Bugsy Siegel's death, Virginia Hill returned all of the missing money to Meyer Lansky.

FADE OUT/FADE IN:

In 1966, In Kopple, Austria, Virginia Hill committed suicide.

FADE OUT/FADE IN:

Las Vegas today — the strip at night — glittering and garish, over which the end titles roll.

THE END

...which sends her, devastated, into the desert night

ABOUT THE AUTHOR

JAMES TOBACK WAS BORN IN 1944 IN NEW YORK CITY, WHERE HE ATTENDED THE
ETHICAL CULTURE SCHOOLS BEFORE MOVING ON TO HARVARD COLLEGE,
FROM WHICH HE GRADUATED IN 1966. HE WAS A LECTURER IN ENGLISH AT THE CITY
COLLEGE OF NEW YORK, A CONTRIBUTOR TO JOURNALS RANGING FROM *ESQUIRE*
TO *DISSENT*, AND AUTHOR OF THE CONTROVERSIAL BIOGRAPHICAL/AUTOBIOGRAHICAL
MEMOIR *JIM* (ABOUT HIMSELF AND JIM BROWN, 1971) WHEN HE BEGAN
A CAREER IN MOVIES WITH THE ORIGINAL SCREENPLAY FOR THE HIGHLY ACCLAIMED
KAREL REISZ FILM *THE GAMBLER* (1974).

TOBACK HAS SINCE WRITTEN AND DIRECTED *FINGERS* (1978), *LOVE AND MONEY* (1982),
EXPOSED (1983), *THE PICK-UP ARTIST* (1987) AND *THE BIG BANG* (1990).

Director Barry Levinson

BUGSY

TriStar Pictures Presents WARREN BEATTY ANNETTE BENING
"BUGSY" HARVEY KEITEL BEN KINGSLEY AND JOE MANTEGNA MUSIC BY ENNIO MORRICONE
WRITTEN BY JAMES TOBACK PRODUCED BY MARK JOHNSON, BARRY LEVINSON AND WARREN BEATTY DIRECTED BY BARRY LEVINSON

FREE!

Citadel Film Series Catalog

From James Stewart to Moe Howard and The Three Stooges, Woody Allen to John Wayne, The Citadel Film Series is America's largest film book library.

Now with more than 125 titles in print, books in the series make perfect gifts—for a loved one, a friend, or yourself!

We'd like to send you, free of charge, our latest full-color catalog describing the Citadel Film Series in depth. To receive the catalog, call 1-800-447-BOOK or send your name and address to:

**Citadel Film Series/Carol Publishing Group
Distribution Center B
120 Enterprise Avenue
Secaucus, New Jersey 07094**

The titles you'll find in the catalog include:
The Films Of...

Alan Ladd
Alfred Hitchcock
All Talking! All Singing!
    All Dancing!
Anthony Quinn
The Bad Guys
Barbara Stanwyck
Barbra Streisand:
    The First Decade
Barbra Streisand:
    The Second Decade
Bela Lugosi
Bette Davis
Bing Crosby
Black Hollywood
Boris Karloff
Bowery Boys
Brigitte Bardot
Burt Reynolds
Carole Lombard
Cary Grant
Cecil B. DeMille
Character People
Charles Bronson
Charlie Chaplin
Charlton Heston
Chevalier
Clark Gable
Classics of the Gangster
    Film
Classics of the Horror Film
Classics of the Silent Screen
Cliffhanger
Clint Eastwood
Curly: Biography of a
    Superstooge
Detective in Film
Dick Tracy
Dustin Hoffman
Early Classics of the
    Foreign Film

Elizabeth Taylor
Elvis Presley
Errol Flynn
Federico Fellini
The Fifties
The Forties
Forgotten Films
    to Remember
Frank Sinatra
Fredric March
Gary Cooper
Gene Kelly
Gina Lollobrigida
Ginger Rogers
Gloria Swanson
Great Adventure Films
Great British Films
Great French Films
Great German Films
Great Romantic Films
Great Science Fiction Films
Great Spy Films
Gregory Peck
Greta Garbo
Harry Warren and the
    Hollywood Musical
Hedy Lamarr
Hello! My Real Name Is
Henry Fonda
Hollywood Cheesecake:
    60 Years of Leg Art
Hollywood's Hollywood
Howard Hughes in Hollywood
Humphrey Bogart
Ingrid Bergman
Jack Lemmon
Jack Nicholson
James Cagney
James Stewart
Jane Fonda
Jayne Mansfield

Jeanette MacDonald and
    Nelson Eddy
Jewish Image in American
    Films
Joan Crawford
John Garfield
John Huston
John Wayne
John Wayne Reference
    Book
John Wayne Scrapbook
Judy Garland
Katharine Hepburn
Kirk Douglas
Lana Turner
Laurel and Hardy
Lauren Bacall
Laurence Olivier
Lost Films of the
    Fifties
Love in the Film
Mae West
Marilyn Monroe
Marlon Brando
Moe Howard and The
    Three Stooges
Montgomery Clift
More Character People
More Classics of the
    Horror Film
More Films of the '30s
Myrna Loy
Non-Western Films of
    John Ford
Norma Shearer
Olivia de Havilland
Paul Newman
Paul Robeson
Peter Lorre
Pictorial History of Science
    Fiction Films

Pictorial History of Sex
    in Films
Pictorial History of War
    Films
Pictorial History of the
    Western Film
Rebels: The Rebel Hero
    in Films
Rita Hayworth
Robert Redford
Robert Taylor
Ronald Reagan
The Seventies
Sex in the Movies
Sci-Fi 2
Sherlock Holmes
Shirley MacLaine
Shirley Temple
The Sixties
Sophia Loren
Spencer Tracy
Steve McQueen
Susan Hayward
Tarzan of the Movies
They Had Faces Then
The Thirties
Those Glorious Glamour Years
Three Stooges Book of Scripts
Three Stooges Book of Scripts,
    Vol. 2
The Twenties
20th Century Fox
Warren Beatty
W. C. Fields
Western Films of John Ford
West That Never Was
William Holden
William Powell
Wood ˙'"
World